Imitate Paul

FIVE KEYS FROM THE APOSTLE FOR EVERY CHURCH PLANTER, LEADER AND BELIEVER

Gary Mayer

I would not be writing this book if it were not for my wonderful wife, Barb. Without her I would never have reached this point in my Christian life. At some time in my 19 years as a pastor I would have thrown in the towel.

Barb has been invaluable in two ways. She was, and still is, my chief encourager and cheerleader. When things were tough, as they inevitably are for all of us, when I doubted myself or wallowed in self-pity, she was there to encourage me and tell me I had what it took.

Secondly, her prophet gifting, although not always welcome, was almost always accurate in helping me discern situations and navigate ministry challenges. When I was naive and blind, she was razor sharp and alert. I have grown to appreciate this very much over the years, which can be a challenge for exhorters like me.

Barb has also consistently encouraged me to write. She believes I have something important to share and it must be written down. The Lord has shown and taught us many things over the years and without her consistent encouragement to write, this book would still be on my to do list.

I also want to thank Pastor Mike Vincent and the church planting team at Calvary Chapel Rosarito. The content of this book has largely come from the teachings I have given to the men who are preparing to go to the mission field planting churches in Mexico and other nations. Pastor Mike's graciousness in including me as part of his teaching team has been a great opportunity to be a part of equipping church planters for the 21st century.

Contents

But none of these things move me; nor do I count my life dear to myself, so that I may finish my race with joy, and the ministry which I received from the Lord Jesus, to testify to the gospel of the grace of God.

Apostle Paul

Preface

I have written this book with church planters, church leaders and missionaries in mind, but the contents pertain equally to every believer, each son and daughter of God.

Imitate Paul is intended to be a companion book to the other excellent church planting books available today. There is first-rate material now available that emphasizes the hows, whats, whys, wheres, and whens of church planting. Much has been learned about successful church planting models and strategies and is now being taught widely. These have been fine-tuned to fit the situation, from the first world and post-Christian cultures of the West to unreached people groups in unimaginably challenging and dangerous nations. This training greatly increases the chances of success for the church planter and will save many from false starts and failures. This aspect of training is indispensable, but there is more that needs to be said.

Biblically speaking, the most important ingredient is the leader himself. Paul is the premier example found in Scripture. It is an understatement to say he is the model church planter. It is one thing to look to Paul and study his methods. It is quite another to study the man himself — his revelation, his teaching, his endurance, his power, his vision and his faith. Indeed, Paul exhorts us to *imitate* him.

We have come through a season, especially here in the West, that emphasizes methods. Methods for successful ministry and leadership are studied and taught through courses, books, blogs, and conferences. The emphasis on methods has at least one weakness — it has marginalized the importance of the power of God working in and through his sons and daughters as the key to successful ministry. In the future, tried and tested methods will be insufficient.

Paul warns Timothy in 2 Timothy 3:1 that we are to be prepared for perilous times to come in the last days — difficult, dangerous, exceedingly fierce times. Seasons of shaking and persecution are in front of us. Paul and the early church experienced this. Now, more than ever, his life needs to be our model. We are privileged to have Paul as our mentor.

It is clear from Scripture that Paul succeeded because God was working powerfully through him. Paul was not discouraged by his many trials. We never see him burned out and he did not quit, but he *finished his race with joy* and fulfilled his calling. You may not be Paul, but you have the same Father, Son, and Holy Spirit. You have the same glorious gospel, the same grace, the same inspired Word of God, and the same power available to you. The lessons of his life will transcend all cultures and all church planting situations.

God gave Moses specific details for building the tabernacle. He gathered a team of skilled workers, provided the leadership, the vision and the plans. When it was finished it was a beautiful, but empty structure — until the presence of God filled the tabernacle.

There is a loose parallel here with church planting methods and strategies, especially as we move forward into the 21st century. The leader can get all the details right — the right location, team, leadership, vision, programs, training, teaching, discipleship and worship. However, this alone can be little more than a well-run *God-business* without the presence, anointing, and power of God operating in the leader and the life of the church.

I have written this book in hopes of better equipping church planters to increase the likelihood of their success, of inspiring existing church leaders who may be discouraged and disheartened, and for all believers who desire to be fruitful in their own callings.

The five keys to Paul's life that I am proposing have been written about in-depth over the years by authors far more capable and eloquent than me. If this book brings additional and important training and discipleship material to the Christian scene it is in the identification of these elements, developing and expressing their importance, and relating them to 21st century life and ministry.

There are discussion questions at the end of each chapter. It is my hope that this book can be useful in a small group setting to encourage and disciple all believers in their quest for maturity and fruitfulness. The subjects covered in Paul's five keys are deep and wide. In this book I am only able to scratch the surface. Take time individually and as a group to dig deep, for there are treasures awaiting.

Gary Mayer

Introduction

I have been a Christian for 47 years and I pastored for 19 of those years. During this time I have always been struck by the gap I see in so many believers' lives, including my own — the gap between the high calling and lofty promises of Scripture and our actual lives lived out in the midst of challenges and trials. I have been on a quest for many years to understand this gap in the hope of seeing my own life more aligned with the promises of Scripture. I long to see God's children live in victory and not defeat, to finish their race with joy and not drop out along the way.

It is often taught that the book of Acts is the model for the church. How much more is the apostle Paul the ultimate example of the successful church planter, church leader and missionary. Twice Paul encourages the believers in Corinth to imitate him. "Therefore I urge you, imitate me" (1 Cor. 4:16). "Imitate me, just as I also imitate Christ" (1 Cor. 11:1). He encourages the believers in Philippi to follow his example (Phil. 3:17), as he also does to the Thessalonians (2 Thess. 3:7, 9). This book is about discovering the keys to his life and ministry so that we can walk in his shoes.

The statistics of suffering pastors are stunning. We will examine this in more detail later, but as one statistic reveals, it is said that for every ten pastors who go into the ministry, only one retires from the ministry in some form! [1]

Something happened to the other nine. Many leave the ministry disillusioned, discouraged, defeated and burned out. Surely this is not God's plan. What is amiss in so many of our lives? What are the ingredients that will empower success and mitigate against failure? What are the antidotes?

In studying Paul's life, we will explore five keys to his success, five foundational truths operating at a core level.

A Certain Calling: Paul had a dramatic encounter with the resurrected Christ on the road to Damascus. It is difficult to over-estimate the importance of every leader being certain of their calling, especially a pioneer and church planter. A certain calling empowers a strong faith that overcomes trials. A lack of the assurance of God's calling makes overcoming faith impossible. Uncertainty sows seeds of destruction in the foundation of any ministry.

A Lasting Vision: Paul states his vision succinctly in Acts 20:24. "But none of these things move me [speaking of his many trials]; nor do I count my life dear to myself, so that I may finish my race with joy, and the ministry which I received from the Lord Jesus, to testify to the gospel of the grace of God."

Paul had a vision that inspired and sustained him. His criterion for success was to *finish his race with joy* and to be faithful with the gifts and calling he had been given. With his eyes firmly on the finish line, he was able to use all the privileges and power of the gospel to finish his race. Unfortunately, many church leaders and future church planters measure their success by *secondary* visions or goals. If for some reason results do not measure up, forces are set in place that eventually lead to weariness, discouragement and defeat. We need to rediscover our *primary* vision for life and ministry.

A Glorious Gospel: Paul lived his life based on the *personal revelation* he received from Jesus. He not only had a dramatic calling, but the eyes of his heart were opened by personal revelation to what he later called "my gospel" in Romans 2:16 and the "glorious gospel" in 1 Timothy 1:11.

The gospel Paul was given was far greater and more expansive than forgiveness of sins and set on a path to heaven. He is careful to develop these doctrines and privileges in his epistles. In Ephesians 1:3 Paul tell us that God has given us "... every spiritual blessing in heavenly places in Christ." In chapter 3 verse 19 he prays for believers that we "... may be filled with all the fullness of God." Paul's writings are saturated with powerful truths like these.

Paul not only taught these truths, he lived them. Yes, he knew them doctrinally and intellectually, but experientially as well. Personal revelation seared them into the DNA of his life. If this were also the testimony of believers today, we would see Paul's victorious life replicated in the lives of countless leaders and believers. Personal revelation is thus an important theme of this book, especially as it relates to Paul's many faceted gospel.

A Strong Finish: Endurance is the necessary ingredient for finishing your race. *Hupomeno* is the Greek word usually translated patience, perseverance or endurance. It is the grit and determination to finish one's task. This is an irreplaceable character trait for any Christian, especially church planters, leaders and missionaries. The Apostle Paul certainly demonstrated this inner strength as he overcame every trial that confronted him. Regardless of what life threw at him, he used every ounce of strength to finish his race with joy and the ministry he had been given by the Lord Jesus.

The endurance to finish our race with joy, as modeled by Paul, is composed of three important ingredients. Each could be a separate chapter, but for simplicity and brevity, I will group them all under the heading of endurance: serving God out of love (not duty), having a right understanding of trials, and developing a strong and vibrant faith.

A Secret Place: The great Apostle knew he had to be filled regularly with the power of God. He gives a one-verse window into his personal and private relationship with the Lord. In 2 Corinthians 4:16 he says, "Therefore we do not lose heart. Even though our outward man is perishing, yet the inward man is being renewed day by day." In John 15 Jesus gave the illustration of the vine and branches. He said the branches (we) need to abide (rest) in the vine (Jesus). When this is a daily occurrence the sap, the essence of divine life, will flow into the branches. Paul discovered this key and indulged daily. We need to imitate him. I believe it was in the secret place that Jesus unveiled many of the revelations Paul taught and experienced personally. It seems that Paul's experience in his secret place transcended what today we have come to call our daily devotions.

All five keys are available to everyone today, no matter what your calling — to plant churches, to lead ministries, to serve in the children's ministry or worship team, to extend God's Kingdom in a secular job or to raise a family as a full-time mother. These five aspects of Paul's life work together to forge a recipe for greatness – greatness in discipleship, in fulfilling God's call on your life, and in finishing your race with joy. They are synergistic. Their combination taken together empowers church planters and leaders to joyously fulfill their callings. They are mandatory if we are to close the gap between our high calling and the experience of so many.

May God answer Paul's prayer for you personally as you read and study this book:

That the God of our Lord Jesus Christ, the Father of glory, may *give to you the spirit of wisdom and revelation in the knowledge of Him, the eyes of your understanding being enlightened*; that you may know what is the hope of His calling, what are the riches of the glory of His inheritance in the saints, and what *is* the exceeding greatness of His power toward us who believe, according to the working of His mighty power (Eph. 1:17-19, emphasis mine).

Let the adventure begin.

CHAPTER 1

A Significant Problem

Everything began well for US Airways Flight 1549 on a cold, partly cloudy afternoon, January 15, 2009. With 150 passengers and five crew onboard, the flight left New York's LaGuardia Airport bound for Charlotte, North Carolina.

All the preparations were made and things were in order. The plane was a trusted Airbus A320, a well-tested model with a good safety record. A veteran pilot, the now famous "Sully" Sullenberger, headed the crew. Sully was a former US Air Force fighter pilot with nearly 20,000 flight hours.

Two minutes into the flight, at an altitude of only 2800 feet, the plane struck a flock of Canada geese, causing both engines to promptly shut down. The plane lost all power and quick decisions had to be made if there were to be any chance of survival.

Most readers will of course know what happened. The scene of Flight 1549 landing on the Hudson River is indelibly etched in our memories. The heroism of Captain Sullenberger and his crew resulted in everyone onboard surviving. The television pictures of passengers standing on the wings and rescue boats hurrying to the scene captivated and thrilled millions of viewers.

Flights like this happen by the thousands around the world every day. They have become routine for most of us but never taken for granted by those responsible for the safety of the passengers. Things don't always go as expected. Ground and aircrew must be trained for every eventuality to be able to respond quickly to unexpected events.

Unfortunately, there is a parallel story for far too many pastors and church planters, not to mention countless believers. At the outset, adventures in faith are exciting — full of potential, promise, and possibilities. Teams are prepared and trained. The captain is excited, plans are in place, and things begin to take off. Seldom do things go as planned. Often we run into engine-threatening geese and we, like Sully Sullenberger must react. What starts out as dreams and visions of answering the call of God, planting churches and extending the Kingdom of God, all too often ends in discouragement, burnout, and abandonment of the mission.

The issue is not so much the challenges themselves, but our response to them and their effect upon us. Jesus warned that we would encounter tribulations and persecutions. Life is full of them. After we become Christians it seems like we suddenly have a target on our back as we come into the crosshairs of the devil's lens. This is especially true of the church planter, church leader and missionary.

The enemy is always opposing the plans of God, the people of God, and the Kingdom of God. An obscure but instructive Old Testament story exposes one of his key strategies. We read about it in 1 Samuel 13. The Philistines and the Israelites were battling constantly. The Philistines employed the unique but effective strategy of removing the blacksmiths from the Israelites. Let's pick up the story in verses 19-22.

> "Now there was no blacksmith to be found throughout all the land of Israel, for the Philistines said, 'Lest the Hebrews make swords or spears.' But all the Israelites would go down to the Philistines to sharpen each man's plowshare, his mattock, his ax, and his sickle; and the charge for a sharpening was a pim for the plowshares, the mattocks, the forks, and the axes, and to set the points of the goads. So it came about, on the day of battle, that there was neither sword nor spear found in the hand of any of the people who were with Saul and Jonathan. But they were found with Saul and Jonathan his son."

The Philistines, by removing the blacksmiths, took away from Israel their ability to farm and wage war. By eliminating the source of the instruments of farming and war, they blunted Israel's fruitfulness and military victories. Blacksmiths were the enablers, those who equipped others to do the work of farming and fighting wars. This is an apt description of today's church leaders (apostles, prophets, evangelists, pastors and teachers) who are called to equip the body of Christ to do the work of ministry (Eph. 4:12).

Today, too, the enemy is focusing on removing the blacksmiths from the body of Christ. If they are deposed the Church's fruitfulness and victorious life will be drastically affected. We need our leaders desperately. We need them to be successful, victorious, and fruitful in their ministry to the body of Christ.

The Gap

The trials of life and the attacks of the enemy, instead of maturing the Christian leader, too often lead to his defeat. On one hand I see troubling statistics, but on the other I see extravagant promises in the Word of God. Why is there this gap between the actual experience of so many and what we read in Scripture? What is missing? Before we investigate some possible answers let's analyze the gap in more detail.

A quick internet search will reveal sizable research into the problem. I don't want to belabor the point but we must get a sense of the issues before we can move on. Here is a sampling. [1]

- 70% of pastors constantly fight depression.
- 50% of pastors feel so discouraged that they would leave the ministry if they could, but have no other way of making a living.
- 50% of ministers starting out will not last 5 years.
- 1 out of every 10 ministers will actually retire as a minister in some form.
- 94% of clergy families feel the pressures of the pastor's ministry.

- 80% of pastors' spouses wish their spouse would choose a different profession.
- Many denominations report an "empty pulpit crisis." They cannot find ministers willing to fill positions.

Behind these statistics are thousands of tragic stories — broken lives, broken dreams, failed marriages, scattered children, damaged faith, and unrealized fruit for the Kingdom of God. This must break the heart of God and encourage the army of Satan.

These statistics are a stark contrast to the promises we find in Scripture. There is no trial, no negative experience a Christian leader could possibly encounter, for which there is not an answer, a strength, a promise, a strategy or a grace from God that will eventually bring victory.

A small sampling of Scripture will demonstrate the gap between the promises to all and the experiences of many. Please read these carefully and allow the life that is within them to sink into your heart.

> My brethren, count it all joy when you fall into various trials, knowing that the testing of your faith produces patience. But let patience have its perfect work, that you may be perfect and complete, lacking nothing (Js. 1:2-4).

> For if by the one man's offense death reigned through the one, much more those who receive abundance of grace and of the gift of righteousness will reign in life through the One, Jesus Christ (Rom. 5:17).

> Grace and peace be multiplied to you in the knowledge of God and of Jesus our Lord, as His divine power has given to us all things that pertain to life and godliness, through the knowledge of Him who called us by glory and virtue, by

which have been given to us his exceedingly great and precious promises, that through these you may become partakers of the divine nature, having escaped the corruption that is in the world through lust. (2 Pet. 1:2-4).

The thief does not come except to steal, and to kill, and to destroy. I have come that they may have life, and that they may have it more abundantly (Jn. 10:10).

I can do all things through Christ who strengthens me (Phil. 4:13).

For everyone who has been born of God overcomes the world. And this is the victory that has overcome the world—our faith (1 Jn. 5:4).

Yet, in all these things we are more than conquerors through him who loved us (Rom. 8:37).

But thanks be to God, who gives us the victory through our Lord Jesus Christ (1 Cor. 15:57).

I say then: Walk in the Spirit, and you shall not fulfill the lust of the flesh (Gal. 5:16).

What shall we say then? Shall we continue in sin that grace may abound? Certainly not! How shall we who died to sin live any longer in it (Rom. 6:1-2)?

Come to Me, all you who labor and are heavy laden, and I will give you rest. Take My yoke upon you and learn from Me, for I am gentle and lowly in heart, and you will find rest for your souls. For My yoke is easy and My burden is light (Matt. 11:28-30).

Rejoice in the Lord always. Again I will say, rejoice! Let your gentleness be known to all men. The Lord is at hand. Be anxious for nothing, but in everything by prayer and supplication, with thanksgiving, let your requests be made known to God; and the peace of God, which surpasses all understanding, will guard your hearts and minds through Christ Jesus (Phil. 4:4-7).

Which of you by worrying can add one cubit to his stature? So why do you worry about clothing? Consider the lilies of the field, how they grow: they neither toil nor spin; and yet

I say to you that even Solomon in all his glory was not arrayed like one of these. Now if God so clothes the grass of the field, which today is, and tomorrow is thrown into the oven, will He not much more clothe you, O you of little faith? Therefore do not worry, saying, 'What shall we eat?' or 'What shall we drink?' or 'What shall we wear?' For after all these things the Gentiles seek. For your heavenly Father knows that you need all these things. But seek first the Kingdom of God and His righteousness, and all these things shall be added to you. Therefore do not worry about tomorrow, for tomorrow will worry about its own things. Sufficient for the day is its own trouble (Matt. 6:27-34).

Now to Him who is able to do exceedingly abundantly above all that we ask or think, according to the power that works in us, to Him *be* glory in the church by Christ Jesus to all generations, forever and ever. Amen (Eph. 3:20-21)

These are stunning truths and staggering promises — all intended to be woven into the fabric of our lives. When compiled together like this, they awaken our hearts to greater possibilities — ones lived out in Paul's life, our mentor and model.

These passages of Scripture are not taken out of context nor are they cherry-picked to exaggerate the message of Scripture. This is the teaching of Jesus and his disciples as to the truth of the gospel, the good news of the message of the Kingdom of God. Paul called this gospel the *glorious gospel.* Truly it is glorious. If taken at face value these promises are above and beyond what we could ever think or imagine. It is filled with power and grace to live this Christian life in such a way that should make the previous statistics of failure null and void.

These promises are not earned. They are not for the special few or for the superstars of the faith. They are part of the spiritual inheritance we receive as a free gift of grace and flow freely from God's heart of love toward all believers.

If the word of God is true, what is the problem? The Apostle Paul, our model church planter, finished his race with joy overcoming every trial, every disappointment, and every attack. Somehow, the three enemies of our soul — the world, the flesh, and the devil, have gained the upper hand in the lives of so many. I would suggest these as some of the possible reasons.

- We believe lies more than the truth.
- We have subtly fallen into legalism, living life out of a sense of dos and don'ts rather than out of love.
- We are weak in faith and weak in appropriating the truths of Scripture.
- We have not received these truths in a personal way; we know the doctrine but it has not become part of our lives.
- We are hearers but not doers of the word.
- We have allowed unrepented sin to remain in our lives.
- We have never grasped, in a personal way, the full extent of the glorious gospel and the indwelling Christ.
- We have somehow blunted the Holy Spirit's power in our lives.
- We have allowed pride to stand in the way of the power of God moving in our lives.
- We are walking more in the strength of our flesh than in the Spirit.
- We trust more in methods than in God himself.

As we can see, there is a disconnect between the promises in the Word of God and the actual life experiences of many. This has tragic results in the lives of our spiritual leaders and their families. Unfortunately, far too many have become casualties on the battlefield of the Christian life. Ministries have been cut short and lives have been shattered.

To use our earlier illustration, the atmosphere of ministry is full of Canada geese. Far too many are unprepared for the impact they make on our lives, families, and ministries. Nevertheless, the Apostle Paul negotiated every goose attack and finished his race with joy. How did he do it? What were the keys to his life and ministry?

The discovery of these five keys is exciting. The possibility of applying them to our lives is a great adventure.

Questions to Consider:

1. We've been looking at the gap between the promises of Scripture and the experience of many Christians. How would you describe this gap in your own life? As you look at this gap now, compare it to how it was a few years ago. Does this encourage you?
2. Be specific and try to identify the gaps in your life. What are your major weaknesses? Ask your spouse or others to give you feedback.
3. Can you see how this gap can lead to failure in your ministry and in your personal Christian walk?
4. How do you feel as you read the promises of Scripture above? In what areas do you find yourself challenged?

5. Using our illustration, can you identify any geese strikes in your life and ministry? How did you respond to the impact? Did you land safely and protect your passengers?

CHAPTER 2

A Certain Calling

Let us begin looking at Paul's life by analyzing his call into the ministry, when he was known as Saul, not Paul.

Saul's life was tipped upside down and turned around on the road to Damascus. You know the story. He was determined to bring back the followers of Jesus to Jerusalem bound in chains. At midday Saul suddenly saw a bright light from heaven, brighter than the sun. He hit the ground trembling and astonished.

In Acts 26 Paul would recall this encounter with Jesus in which he received his lifetime calling:

So I said, 'Who are You, Lord?' And He said, 'I am Jesus, whom you are persecuting. But rise and stand on your feet; for I have appeared to you for this purpose, to make you a minister and a witness both of the things which you have seen and of the things which I will yet reveal to you. I will deliver you from the Jewish people, as well as from the Gentiles, to whom I now send you, to open their eyes, in order to turn them from darkness to light, and from the power of Satan to God, that they may receive forgiveness of sins and an inheritance among those who are sanctified by faith in Me' (Acts 26:15-18).

Paul later summarized his calling this way: "But none of these things move me; nor do I count my life dear to myself, so that I may finish my race with joy, and the ministry which I received from the Lord Jesus, to testify to the gospel of the grace of God" (Acts 20:24).

It is difficult to overstate the importance of knowing with certainty that your ministry is the result of a call from God. Notice Jesus' exact words to Saul: "I have appeared to you for this purpose, to make you a minister and a witness both of the things which you have seen and of the things which I will yet reveal to you."

Jesus appeared to Saul in order to make him a minister and a witness. In the book of Acts we see Paul giving his personal testimony many times. He not only preached the gospel Jesus revealed to him, but his encounter with the risen Jesus became a central part of his personal testimony.

When trials, opposition, disappointments, betrayal, and persecutions of every sort hit your life, when everything around you screams, "Quit!" the certainty of your calling is an anchor, a stabilizing force to keep you from faltering. It is a solid foundation that supports your ministry when the winds of adversity try to blow it away. When the devil whispers to you, "Hath God said?" you are able to rebut him by proclaiming with confidence and certainty, "Yes, God hath said!"

When your confidence is shaken you are able to continue on knowing God called you into the ministry.

Paul's encounter on the Damascus Road became an integral part of his witness. This is as it should be. A personal testimony is not only personal, it is powerful. It changes you and it will influence and change others as they hear how you and God had an encounter. We find these defining moments throughout Scripture — men like Abraham, Isaac, Jacob, Joseph, Moses, Joshua and the prophets in the Old Testament; the apostles, Cornelius, Mary and the woman at the well in the New Testament. Some testimonies are miraculous like Paul's on the Damascus Road, while some are more ordinary.

Altars

When these men and women encountered God they often built altars as a memorial to commemorate their experience, like Jacob did at Bethel (Gen. 35:7). In my life, I have come to call these transformative encounters with God my personal *altars*. In Exodus 20:24 God told the children of Israel to "Build my altars wherever I cause my name to be remembered, and I will come to you and bless you" (NLT). Of course, I don't actually gather stones into a pile when God reveals something to me — these are spiritual altars I build in my heart and mind. They become a very important part of my personal testimony and are significant in forging my walk with God.

As I look in the rearview mirror at my personal journey with God, I see these altars strategically placed along my path. They are huge milestones marking places where God changed me. Some were encounters with him, usually as the Holy Spirit quickened the Word of God to my heart in a powerful way; some were prophetic words he gave me through friends and strangers alike; some were dynamic encounters with the Word of God whereby I received personal revelation of a gospel truth; and some were major instances of obedience and resultant breakthroughs. Without these defining moments, I could never have become the man of God he wanted. None, however, were more important than the call into full-time ministry.

This significant altar in my life occurred in Paris, France in 1989. Although my calling was not as dramatic as Paul's on the Damascus Road, it was nevertheless life-changing. It happened suddenly and unexpectedly as I walked out the front door of our apartment early on a Saturday morning. I was on the way to our local French patisserie to purchase a treat for breakfast — an unlikely time to hear from heaven. Suddenly, I heard what I still believe was the audible voice of God saying (I remember the exact words), "Gary, you are not listening." These were not comforting words by any means! I was shaken to the core of my soul. I shook and trembled inside for weeks.

Needless to say, I began to listen! Before long I had a sense of what the Lord was saying to me. I knew this was a serious matter, so at my request, my wife and I sat down for a serious discussion. She said, "You go first." (A wise wife!) I told her three things I felt God was saying to me. After each one she responded, "Yes." God was not only speaking to me, he had been speaking to Barb as well. We both received the same message — I was to leave my business career after 21 years, return to England where we had previously lived, go to Bible College, and prepare to pastor.

Many years later, the certainty of my calling played an instrumental role in keeping a storm-ravaged life and ministry afloat. Despite circumstances that were often difficult, I never doubted my calling. I knew that no matter what came my way God would be with me, encouraging me, and providing ample grace to be victorious.

I want to emphasize the importance of my wife hearing from the Lord and confirming my calling. If you are married, it is essential your spouse is fully on-board with your calling. For those 19 years Barb was my biggest encourager and remains so to this day. Together we experienced the truth of Ecclesiastes 4:9-12.

Two are better than one,
Because they have a good reward for their labor.
For if they fall, one will lift up his companion.
But woe to him who is alone when he falls,
For he has no one to help him up.
Again, if two lie down together, they will keep warm;
But how can one be warm alone?
Though one may be overpowered by another, two can withstand him.
And a threefold cord is not quickly broken

A number of years after the call into full-time ministry, I wrote in my spiritual notebook that I had a threefold cord supporting and strengthening me during the difficult times.

- the certainty of my calling
- the encouragement of my wife
- the intercession of Jesus (Rom. 8:34)

My friend, being certain of your calling is indispensable if you are to finish your race with joy and the ministry you have been given. Without this the inevitable trials of ministry may lead you to the point of asking yourself, *Hath God said? Has he really called me?*

If you are sensing God's call on your life to be a church planter or future church leader you need to be certain of your calling. How do you do that? It is probably not recommended that you get on a plane to Israel, find your way to the Damascus Road, and see if Jesus knocks you to the ground! In fact, your situation may be very different from Paul's and mine.

Paul and I were similar in one important way. In each case God needed to get our attention and change the course of our lives — a major U-turn. To do that it was necessary to intervene in a dramatic way. Frankly this is not the best situation, nor the most common.

You may have had a desire to go in the direction of your calling for many years. God has not needed to turn you around but to encourage you in the way you are going. Maybe the call has been a seed growing, developing, and maturing for a very long time. At the deepest heart level God has had a call on your life for as long as you can remember.

In discerning the call of God, there is no standard template to apply to every individual situation. There are however some tried and trusted elements that warrant attention. In Darrin Patrick's book, *Church Planter, The Man, The Message, The Mission,* he looks historically at church fathers' perspectives on callings and summarizes them into three aspects of discerning your calling — the heart confirmation, the head confirmation, and the skill confirmation. [1] Each of these three areas must be considered.

A God-given and initiated calling is at a heart level. The call must touch your heart and kindle a passion in your soul. If you are considering planting a church or going to the mission field, is this something that you know in your heart? At the deepest level of your soul, is your heart telling you this is God's purpose for your life?

The head confirmation is crucial because Jesus taught us to count the cost of any endeavor before proceeding. You need your heart and your mind to be in agreement. You should not sacrifice the practical aspects of godly wisdom on the altar of an excited heart. Both are very important in ascertaining the call of God.

The skill level is more nuanced because you can develop and hone your skills with practice and instruction. Nevertheless, there must be a level of gifting for teaching, pastoring, and leading. Take every opportunity available to you to use and develop these skills. Do others confirm you have a gifting in these areas?

Being certain of your calling brings purpose to your life. Purpose in turn will bring passion, energy, and fulfillment. Jesus was born for a purpose, to bear witness of the truth. "Are You a king then?" Jesus answered, "You say rightly that I am a king. For this cause [purpose] I was born, and for this cause I have come into the world, that I should bear witness to the truth. Everyone who is of the truth hears My voice" (John 18:37, emphasis mine). Jesus was born to die, born to bring redemption and hope to a lost world.

Paul discovered his purpose in life when he encountered Jesus on the Damascus Road. He was to take the gospel of grace to the Gentile world. This purpose gave him the direction, the focus, and the energy to fulfill his calling with joy. Knowing his purpose, Paul had supernatural strength to endure hardship and not become discouraged with the many trials he faced. "Purpose empowers perseverance." [2]

For some of us God must get our attention and turn us around. This kind of calling may involve some fireworks. For others it is a quiet development of something on the inside. Having said that, I want to warn against trying to reason your way into a sense of God's calling and knowing your purpose in life. It best comes from an encounter with him, whether that is dramatic or subtle; suddenly or over an extended period of time.

Sometimes there are blocks that act as obstacles in our hearing the voice of God in important matters, like our calling. One that should always be considered is the question of God's will versus my will. In the life of all serious Christians, there comes a time of full surrender to God – the surrender of us running our lives and turning all matters over to him. Fear is often the reason Christians hold tight control of the reins of their lives. "Can God be trusted?" "God might take me into matters that are fearful for me." These issues must be dealt with so fear and control are no longer blockages. This total surrender can be costly and painful. Andrew Murray calls it *Absolute Surrender* in his book of this title. Paul gets to the heart of the matter in Galatians: "I have been crucified with Christ; it is no longer I who live, but Christ lives in me; and the *life* which I now live in the flesh I live by faith in the Son of God, who loved me and gave Himself for me." This is the work of the cross *in* the life of a believer.

When a mature believer has come to the place of regular surrender to God, they are more able hear and follow the leading of the Lord. Psalm 32:8 says, "I will instruct you and teach you in the way you should go; I will guide you with My eye." God is seeking for each of us to come to the place where we are able to look him in the eye and be moved and guided in that personal intimate relationship. A slight move of his eye will easily guide us as we have yielded hearts inclined toward him.

Either way, if you are like Paul (and me) and you need a serious attention-getter, or you have been slowly receiving your call for years, you need to be certain of your calling. No one is exempt from the trials and pressures that will come, and the devil speaking his lies and temptations. You need to be able to say to yourself, "It is written in my heart by the call of almighty God. I will finish my race with joy and the ministry I have been given by the Lord."

Hebrews 11:6 says, "But without faith it is impossible to please Him, for he who comes to God must believe that He is, and that He is a rewarder of those who diligently seek Him." Diligently seek him. Don't be lazy or presumptuous about such a serious matter. Seek him until you know that you know he is placing this calling upon your life.

It is often recommended that you seek the counsel of others — your pastor, mentors, leaders, friends, and your spouse. Of course, this is true. There is wisdom in many counselors. But this must be said: if their word is a substitute for not hearing God for yourself, when the storms hit, your anchor will not be steadfast. You need to hear for yourself. Let their advice and counsel be confirming words.

My friend, you too need to be able to look into the rearview mirror of your life and examine your own altars — your history of encounters with God. None is more important than the certainty of your calling. Spend the time necessary to be assured of your calling.

In Colossians 1 the great apostle prays a prayer that is on target regarding our first key in Paul's life and ministry — the certainty of one's calling.

> For this reason we also, since the day we heard it, do not cease to pray for you, and to ask that you may be *filled with the knowledge of His will in all wisdom and spiritual understanding*; that you may walk worthy of the Lord, fully pleasing Him, being fruitful in every good work and increasing in the knowledge of God; strengthened with all might, according to His glorious power, for all patience and longsuffering with joy; giving thanks to the Father who has qualified us to be partakers of the inheritance of the saints in the light (v. 9-12, emphasis mine).

From this prayer of Paul's, you can be assured it is the Father's will for you to be certain of your calling. It is not his desire that you be uncertain or double-minded. Oh, the certainty may come over time of course, but if it is of God, it will come.

Faith

Knowing your call with certainty fuels your faith to carry out your ministry with perseverance and power. This idea was woven into my discussion above, but I want to draw your attention to it further. It is not possible to be a good leader and be weak in faith. This matter of faith is indispensable.

A reading of Hebrews 11 reminds us that men and women of faith did great exploits. As a sampling, let's look at verses 32-34. "And what more shall I say? For the time would fail me to tell of Gideon and Barak and Samson and Jephthah, also of David and Samuel and the prophets: who through faith subdued kingdoms, worked righteousness, obtained promises, stopped the mouths of lions, quenched the violence of fire, escaped the edge of the sword, out of weakness were made strong, became valiant in battle, turned to flight the armies of the aliens."

It takes little imagination to see how these phrases can be applied to modern-day ministry. Church planters, leaders, and missionaries have spiritual battles that parallel victories fought and won by these Old Testament saints. Battles are won not so much by using tried and tested methods, but by strong faith.

Let's go a little deeper.

From Paul's description of the armor of God in Ephesians 6, we know that faith acts as a shield against all the fiery darts of the enemy (vs. 16). When Satan's strategy is to discourage you and cause you to quit, the faith that results from the certainty of your calling extinguishes those fiery darts. But there is more.

We also know from verse 17 that we are to take the sword of the Spirit, which is the Word of God, and deal a deathblow to the enemy and his strategies. The Greek word used here for *word*, is *rhema*, which means "something that is spoken clearly, vividly, in unmistakable terms and undeniable language. In the New Testament, the word *rhema* carries the idea of a quickened word." (3) The word *sword* here in verse 17 describes a short sword, shaped like a dagger and razor sharp on both sides. It was used by the Roman soldier for stabbing at close range and was a lethal weapon dreaded by his enemies.

Let's now consider Hebrews 4:12. Here the writer to the Hebrews says, "For the word of God is living and powerful, and sharper than any two-edged sword ..." Rick Renner, in his excellent book, *Sparkling Gems from the Greek*, brings out and applies the Greek meaning of this two-edged sword. It is very relevant to our topic at hand — the certainty of your calling.

Renner tells us that the Greek word here for two-edged is formed from two words, literally meaning *two-mouthed*! We also see this same language used in Revelation 1:16, with a two-edged sword coming out of Jesus' mouth. So, the Word of God is like a sword with two edges. It is first spoken by God and is the logos, or written Word of God (used in Hebrews 4:12), which puts one sharp edge on the sword. Then, when it is quickened to us personally and becomes a *rhema* word to us, a second razor sharp side is added when you know it and speak it. This is the sword of the Spirit spoken of in Ephesians 6:17 that we are to use to defeat the enemy. [3]

When you are certain of your calling, when God has spoken it to you in a *rhema* word, you have a weapon like a stabbing Roman sword to speak against the discouraging, deceiving lies of Satan, just like Jesus did in Luke 4. When the enemy assaults you in the midst of trials with "Hath God said?" you are able to respond, using the sword of the Spirit, the certainty of your calling. When the enemy uses contrary circumstances, unmet expectations, or fiery trials to tempt you to throw in the towel, you are able to resist him standing strong in faith. You will be able to endure to the end and finish the race God has given you to run.

This is what Paul is teaching his spiritual son, Timothy, when he tells him, "This charge I commit to you, son Timothy, according to the prophecies previously made concerning you, that by them you may wage a good warfare," (1 Tim. 1:18). Timothy had obviously received personal prophecies concerning his life and ministry. Paul is teaching Timothy that these words from God enable Timothy to stand strong and fulfill his calling. They empower him to fight the good fight, to wage a good warfare against all opposition. May this encourage you my reader, as well.

The certainty of your calling has one very important application for every Christian, not just church leaders and church planters – the certainty of your salvation. Our salvation is the most important calling in our lives. The certainty of your salvation has a critical application to everything I've written in this chapter. Some Christians have doubts and these doubts are an open door to the enemy to accuse and attack your faith. If you are truly born again, there should be a certainty in your heart and mind that is a foundation undergirding your faith to overcome every trial of life. In 1 John 5:13, the Apostle John writes: "These things I have written to you who believe in the name of the Son of God, *that you may know* that you have eternal life, and that you may continue to believe in the name of the Son of God" (emphasis mine). My friend, you are to be certain of your calling unto eternal life.

There at least five ways you can know for sure you have been born again and are certain of eternal life.

1. You have a desire to obey the Word and walk in the light. (See 1 John 2:3, 2:29, 3:10, 5:2-3).
2. You have a love of the brethren. (See 1 John 1:7, 3:14, 4:7-8, 12).
3. You have a witness of the Spirit. (See 1 John 3:24, 4:13, 5:10; Romans 8:16-17; Ephesians 1:13).
4. The confession of Jesus. (See 1 John 2:23, 4:15, 5:1).
5. A changed life; a personal testimony. (See 2 Corinthians 5:17; Ephesians 4:22-24; Galatians 5:22-23; Acts 26:1-32).

If you are ever plagued by doubts of your salvation, please take the time to carefully go through these Scriptures to be certain of your calling unto eternal life. This is the first step in imitating Paul.

A Final Word

In this chapter I made the certainty of your calling a very important matter. Over and over I emphasized how critical this matter is. Paul's calling was sure and certain.

Having said that, it must also be said that following Jesus is risky business! I do not mean to say that being certain of your calling removes all risks. By their very nature, obeying the call of God, and responding to the promptings of the Holy Spirit, carry a certain amount of risk. Jesus did what he saw the Father doing (John 5:19-20). He saw clearly, but we see more dimly. Each of us must evaluate our calling and the risks involved. That is the life of faith. If you believe you have heard from God in this matter, go for it. Be bold. Get out of the boat. The Christian life is meant to be an adventure.

Let us now turn to the second of our keys from Paul's life, a vision that will stand the test of time.

Questions to Consider:

1. If you are considering planting a church, how certain are you of your calling? What will you do to make sure of it and/or confirm it?
2. How would you describe your calling — a dramatic, get-your-attention calling or a quiet development of something that has been in your heart for years?
3. Consider this idea of altars in your life. Do you have a history with God in which you can identify these special times of encounter and revelation? If yes, re-

view them today and rejoice. Can you see how he has been leading you up to this point in your life?

4. Have you explored thoroughly and applied personally the three areas involved in confirmation of your calling — the heart, the head, and your skills? Does your heart confirm it? Have your counted the cost? Do your skills provide a foundation for further development? What actions can you take to test your gifts and skills?

5. Have you fully surrendered to God? Can you identify with Paul in Galatians 2:20? If not, let this season of life be the time. Perhaps this will be an altar building moment between you and the Lord.

6. Are you certain of your salvation; your calling unto eternal life? Do you know anyone who is plagued by doubts? Use this time to become certain.

7. Realistically assess your faith. Is it strong? Is it growing? Can you attest to a time when you know God has spoken to you?

8. How would you apply this chapter to other callings in life: business life, housewife, etc.?

CHAPTER 3

A Lasting Vision

The importance of vision is well understood and widely accepted. The power of a vision enables an athlete to endure a strict and arduous training regimen in order to reach his or her goals. Setting the right vision and goals in the business world empowers an organization to co-ordinate all its various parts to work together to accomplish its targets. It is the same in every walk of life, segment of society, and individual endeavor.

A great vision statement, in very few words, is filled with implied possibilities that apply to many aspects of the organization – rich with unsaid, but intended applications. Recently, when visiting a fast food restaurant, I had occasion to peer through the window of their back office and saw on their bulletin board their mission statement. It was placed in clear sight for every employee to see when they arrived at work. It was only three words, but powerful, inspiring, and applied to each employee and every aspect of their business:

"Delight Our Guest." Can you see how this would motivate each employee to the goal of delighted customers? You could apply it to the person who greeted us, the order taker, the cooks, the quality of the food, the cleanliness, the smiles, the attitudes – every person and every aspect of work in this restaurant; all in three words. This idea, these three words permeated into every detail of their business. I was so impressed.

Writing church vision and mission statements has also become widespread in recent years. Excellent material has been written to enable churches to write effective vision statements — inspiring, empowering, clear and memorable. Vision statements often serve an important purpose in enabling a church to move forward together in unity toward a goal that has been inspired by God.

Most experts in this field would agree that a good vision statement should be short and sweet, ideally one sentence, so it is easily memorized. A church's vision is effective and powerful when it becomes part of the DNA of the church — when church leaders and various programs align their activities and energies with the vision and when the entire church is excited and motivated by it.

However, what about the individual pastor, church planter, or missionary? What about every son and daughter of God? Less is written and understood about this. Have you worked through and crafted a personal vision or mission statement? Do you know anyone who has?

This brings us to the second of Paul's keys to his life and ministry. As I study the life of the apostle Paul, I have come to believe that his personal vision was at the heart of his immense success. Paul had something burning in the core of his being that fueled his life and empowered him to overcome every obstacle. He had a vision, a goal, that he was tenacious in pursuing to completion. He knew his God-given purpose.

Paul's vision fulfilled all the criteria for an effective vision statement: inspiring, empowering, clear and memorable. It is short and sweet, one sentence and easily memorized. It is declared in Acts 20:24, as Paul met with the Ephesian elders on his way to Jerusalem. I believe this best summarizes what we would call today, Paul's vision statement.

> "But none of these things move me; nor do I count my life dear to myself, so *that I may finish my race with joy*, and the ministry which I received from the Lord Jesus, to testify to the gospel of the grace of God" (emphasis mine).

I love this statement. I have adopted it as my own personal vision statement. In fact, in 1994, I was personally given this verse as a prophetic word, inspired by the Holy Spirit. It has become embedded in the core of my being.

Paul's vision is helpful for every believer, not just church leaders. Life is busy and full of activities for everyone and for every season of life — raising families, jobs and careers. A vision like Paul's will raise you above the daily and monthly cycles of life to see the big picture. It will keep you on the most important course when you are being pulled to and fro with endless tasks. It will bring fresh air and perspective when you most need it. It can breathe life into endless days of routine.

The heart of this statement in Acts 20:24 is this: "that I may finish my race with joy." This eight word statement is much like the three word mission statement of the fast food restaurant – it rich and full of potential with unsaid but intended applications. It applies to every believer, every day, and in every season of life. It is both present and future oriented. It is lifting and positive, bringing out the best in all of us. It permeates into relationships, trials, attitudes, and priorities.

Let's look at the entirety of this verse in more depth. The first two phrases, "But none of these things move me, nor do I count my life dear to myself," refer back to the previous two verses where Paul explains that the Holy Spirit testified that chains and tribulations awaited him in Jerusalem.

We find examples in Acts 21:4 and 21:11. After Paul left the Ephesian elders from Miletus, he journeyed toward Jerusalem, stopping seven days in Tyre. There, Scripture says of the disciples "They told Paul, through the Spirit not to go up to Jerusalem." Undaunted, Paul then moved on to Caesarea and entered the house of Philip the evangelist. Agabus, a prophet from Judea, "Took Paul's belt, bound his own hands and feet, and said, 'Thus says the Holy Spirit, 'So shall the Jews at Jerusalem bind the man who owns this belt, and deliver him into the hands of Gentiles.'"

Paul's vision statement acknowledges a very important aspect of his life and ministry — he would have to endure trials, beatings, imprisonments and persecutions. This did not surprise him. Interestingly, back in Acts 9:16, Jesus warned him that trials would be a theme of his life when he said, "For I [Jesus] will show him [Paul] how many things he must suffer for My name's sake." By including this in his vision statement Paul is acknowledging a pivotal aspect of his life — none of these trials will move him. He is determined to finish his race regardless of what happens along the line, even losing his life for the gospel.

In this phrase, Paul acknowledges the possibility of losing his life, "... nor do I count my life dear to myself." This attitude is prevalent today in parts of the world where severe persecution is a constant reality, as it was in the early church. This is not so much the case for us who live in the West, at least not yet. Are you so sold out for Jesus that you will die for him? Perhaps, but this will probably remain a theoretical question for most of us.

More relevant for most of us is the practical aspect of the work of the cross *in* our lives. The cross has become an adorning piece of jewelry identifying us as Christians, when it actually is a terrible instrument of death. So, the more relevant question to consider is this — have you died to self? Have you died to your own pride, ego, expectations, flesh, reputation, and self-righteousness? Jesus says in Luke 9:23-24, "If anyone desires to come after Me, let him deny himself, and take up his cross daily, and follow Me. For whoever desires to save his life will lose it, but whoever loses his life for My sake will save it."

This matter may hold a key to reversing the trend of disheartening statistics for pastors and ministers in America and elsewhere. It was a vital aspect of Paul's life. Paul goes into more detail in Philippians 3, verses 1-16.

Paul begins this passage with the theme that he has no confidence in the flesh, no confidence in his own pedigree (as a Pharisee), in his own strength, talents, abilities, or righteousness. As we see later in the passage and in Paul's other writings, it is all about Christ in Paul and Paul in Christ. It is about the power of God working in and through him.

Paul counted everything in his life other than Christ to be rubbish (verse 8). His goal was to "... know Him [Christ] and the power of His resurrection, and the fellowship of His sufferings, being conformed to His death" (verse 10).

The work of the cross can be a painful process as it works deep into the soul, yet at the same time is very liberating as everything is fully surrendered to the Lord. For Paul, as well as for you and me, the cross is key to living in victory and power. It was key to Paul's ministry of power. Notice what he says in 1 Corinthians 2:1-5:

And I, brethren, when I came to you, did not come with excellence of speech or of wisdom declaring to you the testimony of God. For I determined not to know anything among you except Jesus Christ and Him crucified. I was with you in weakness, in fear, and in much trembling. And my speech and my preaching were not with persuasive words of human wisdom, but in demonstration of the Spirit and of power, that your faith should not be in the wisdom of men but in the power of God.

Can you see the work of the cross in Paul's life here? The great apostle of the New Testament, who was weak in fear and in much trembling, had replaced the strong-willed, know-it-all Saul. His preaching and speech were not smooth and powerful. Paul was a humble, totally surrendered man. He had been delivered from self and ego (Gal. 2:20). This is good news, even great news. This is something to shout from the mountaintops, especially for a pastor and church leader. Why? 1 Corinthians 2:4 goes on to say, "... but in demonstration of the Spirit and of power, that your faith should not be in the wisdom of men but in the power of God." This is what we all should want. The work of the cross in you is the road to power and victory.

A.W. Tozer sums this up in his unique way, by saying, "The degree of blessing enjoyed by any man will correspond exactly with the completeness of God's victory over him." [1]

There is another wonderful aspect of this work of the cross in us that we can all celebrate: dead men and women do not sin, do not get easily offended, wallow in self-pity, or feel rejection! This is good news. The work of the cross brings victory over sin. (See Romans 6).

When God spoke to me so powerfully in Paris and changed the direction of my life from a successful business career with its security and benefits, to a life totally surrendered to his will and purpose, this passage in Philippians 3 became very personal. In every area of my life I had to wrestle with God and myself in order to fully surrender to him. The work of the cross dug deep into my inner motivations, expectations, and purpose in life. Total surrender was very painful. I knew there would be no looking back. I was being forced to count the cost.

Although I was not considering the possibility of physical death that Paul referred to in his vision statement, I had to embrace the same total surrender Paul made. This became part of my own testimony and vision statement. This is a mandatory step for every leader (and believer) in order to live victoriously. God will go to great lengths and use every circumstance to kill you! As Tozer asked, has God had his victory over you?

Finishing Your Race ...

Let's move on to the next phrase in Paul's vision statement, "... so that I may finish my race with joy." This, to me, is at the heart of Paul's great success in overcoming every obstacle. Paul has his eyes set on the final goal. Like an athlete his eyes were on the finish line. This is a common theme in Scripture. Look at Hebrews 12:1-2:

> "Therefore we also, since we are surrounded by so great a cloud of witnesses, let us lay aside every weight, and the sin which so easily ensnares us, and let us run with endurance the race that is set before us, looking unto Jesus, the author and finisher of our faith, who for the joy that was set before Him endured the cross, despising the shame, and has sat down at the right hand of the throne of God."

This passage in Hebrews is so closely aligned with Paul's vision statement that I wonder if perhaps both Scriptures came from the heart of the same man. (Did Paul write Hebrews?) Regardless of that debate, we see in this passage an athlete entering a stadium cheered on by multitudes who have gone before, the cheers bringing encouragement to endure to the end. Jesus is given as the great example to overcome every obstacle, even death on a cross, keeping his eye on the joy of heaven. It is interesting that Jesus himself gave a similar testimony to Paul's in John 17:4: "I have glorified You on the earth. I have finished the work which You have given Me to do." Both Paul and Jesus gave testimony to the supreme importance of finishing their race and accomplishing their assignments.

In the days of the early church, persecution and death were ever-present realities. It was so prevalent that *endurance* was called the "queen of all virtues." [2] Endurance was such an important part of Paul's vision I have appointed it one of his five keys to success and I will dedicate an entire chapter to it later.

... With Joy

In his vision statement, Paul did not merely say he was determined to finish his race, but to finish his race *with joy*. This is not a small matter. This adds a new dimension to the idea of endurance. It is one thing to finish a race grimacing in pain; it is quite another to finish the race with joy. It is one thing to endure the race, it is another to enjoy the ride. One is driven by circumstances, the other enjoys the process in spite of circumstances.

This is very meaningful to me. God has encouraged me in my ministry over the years by giving me many prophetic words. One of the principle themes has been this subject of joy. Psalm 100 was highlighted to me over and over by the Lord. May it encourage you as well.

Make a joyful shout to the Lord, all you lands!
Serve the Lord with gladness;
Come before His presence with singing.
Know that the Lord, He is God;
It is He who has made us, and not we ourselves;
We are His people and the sheep of His pasture.

Enter into His gates with thanksgiving,
And into His courts with praise.
Be thankful to Him, and bless His name.
For the Lord is good;
His mercy is everlasting,
And His truth endures to all generations.

Read this over slowly and let the sweet spirit of it sink into your soul. Paul must have worked this Psalm into the DNA of his life and ministry. Maybe he and Silas were singing this Psalm while imprisoned in the Philippian jail.

This matter of joy is very important to the Lord. We read of the Israelites constantly complaining to Moses (and to God) during their 40 years in the desert following their freedom from slavery in Egypt. They suffered many things of course and we can understand their situation, in a measure. Many of us complain about far smaller matters. But how did God view their complaining?

In Deuteronomy 28:47-48 we see how their complaining resulted in God's judgment on the Israelites. "Because you *did not serve the Lord your God with joy and gladness of heart*, for the abundance of everything, therefore you shall serve your enemies, whom the Lord will send against you, in hunger, in thirst, in nakedness, and in need of all things; and He will put a yoke of iron on your neck until He has destroyed you" (emphasis mine).

I know we live under a better covenant now. Nevertheless, we must know that complaining about our circumstances is not pleasing to him. As we think about it, there are two sides to the coin.

First, as a father, he wants what is best for us. Surely this means we are joyful sons and daughters. This is every parent's desire for their children. Nothing would please him more, as a father, than to see us serve him with joy and gladness of heart. There are two ways of achieving this. God could have arranged life on earth so that we would never have any problems and everything would be perfect. Even better, however, is that there is a joy available to us that transcends life's problems. This is what I most admire in Paul. He came to a place in Christ where he was joyful in spite of his trials. This is God's will for each of us.

This coin has another side. Our attitude and demeanor reflect the care and love of our heavenly Father. As a wife reflects her husband's care and love, so our lives reflect upon him and his reputation. It is not only our holiness that reflects upon him, but our joy and gladness of heart. After all, the fruit of the Spirit is joy, not murmuring, heaviness, or sadness.

Jesus quoted from Isaiah 61:1-2a on the Sabbath in Nazareth. That passage goes on in verse 3 to continue to speak of the times of the Messiah and highlights what we are speaking about. "To console those who mourn in Zion, To give them beauty for ashes, The oil of joy for mourning, The garment of praise for the spirit of heaviness; That they may be called trees of righteousness, The planting of the Lord, that He may be glorified" (Is. 61:3).

Many church leaders and believers alike live and labor under a heavy yoke — a spirit of heaviness. This passage is a wonderful promise for you today — that you can receive the oil of joy and a garment of praise replacing the spirit of heaviness. In the context of the entire New Testament, this is a promise that can be yours.

Notice also the last phrase in this verse, "... that He may be glorified." Your life is to be lived in such a way that God is glorified. There is no better way than to serve him with joy and gladness of heart. Concern for his reputation should be preeminent in our lives.

In order to live lives above circumstances, in the power of the Holy Spirit and bearing the fruit of joy, we need to have strong faith — a tangible, living, significant faith. This faith is a confident trust born out of a certainty of your calling and a loving God working all things together for good and for his purposes. This faith will raise you above circumstances. I will expand this significantly in a later chapter about being rightly related to trials.

One time, many years ago, I was going through an especially difficult stretch in my life. I was riding the ups and downs of ministry, allowing circumstances to dictate my level of joy. On the spur of the moment, my wife suggested we attend a 3-day conference in London as a refreshing break — a time to get a little perspective on life. Little did we know that this conference would become a turning point in our lives. Because of the content of the conference and the leading of the Holy Spirit, we made a conscious decision to be happy. Those were the words we used at the time — to be happy —

to be happy regardless of circumstances. We made a decision that our joy would not be controlled by others, or conditions within the ministry. This was a milestone, one of those *altars* I spoke of earlier.

Maybe you are at a low place in your life. Today, with the grace of Jesus and the power of the Holy Spirit, you can make a decision to be happy, to allow the fruit of joy to arise in your heart, to put on a garment of praise for the spirit of heaviness. Let your faith empower you to live above the trials of life.

Let's move on to the last part of Paul's vision in Acts 20:24, "... and the ministry which I received from the Lord Jesus, to testify to the gospel of the grace of God." Here Paul states that he is committed to finish the ministry that Jesus gave him years earlier on the Damascus Road. Jesus gave him his ministry and he was determined to finish his assignment. Period. Paul taught every aspect of the gospel but at the heart, to both Jew and Gentile, was grace. This was his assigned message and he carried it out faithfully to the end. He never lost sight of grace, even when dealing with issues and problems in his letters to the churches.

What an example this is for each of us, whether church planter, pastor, or believer. "For we are His workmanship, created in Christ Jesus for good works, which God prepared beforehand that we should walk in them" (Eph. 2:10). My friend, you have a destiny, a calling from God. He has much for you to do in the Kingdom of God before you go home to be with him. We are all called, we all have a ministry, and we all need to finish our race with joy. "The end of a thing is better than its beginning" (Eccl. 7:8). Period.

Primary and Secondary Visions

With this brief look at Paul's vision statement, I want to highlight a major lesson we need to learn here. I want to contrast what I will call *inferior* vision statements to Paul's vision as stated in Acts 20:24. By *inferior* I do not mean unimportant, but subservient to a higher vision. The lesser should be submitted to the greater. There are primary visions and there are secondary visions. Let me explain by using a recent athletic achievement.

As I write this chapter, John Beeden, 53, has just completed the first non-stop crossing of the Pacific Ocean, from North America to Australia — in a rowboat! Rowing 15 hours a day for 209 days, he traveled over 7000 miles in the most adverse conditions imaginable. He fought daily against weather, current, wind, waves and exhaustion. Few of us could imagine accomplishing a feat like this.

Reading his daily blog is inspiring and instructional. An important part of his strategy was to have daily goals, usually set in nautical miles (nm). Here is an excerpt from his diary, 28 September, 2015.

So I left you at 1830, I had 9.5 hours to do 20.5nm. Normally at 2.5 knots I'd do it by doing 2 x 4.5 hour rows and a break in between. I decided to go to ten hours, so off I go. The wind was still SE and low (a headwind), the water choppy, it was still very frustrating. I couldn't get two oars in the water at the same time to save my life, I just had to grind away. The Sun is full on, no clouds at all now, in fact everything had gone north and there was a long line of cloud west to east clearly identify the equator which was a pretty cool thing to see. Anyway, 5 hours later I've got me 10.5nm but I'm exhausted, I need at least a fifteen minute break. I fill up my water bottles, grab some boiled sweats (pure sugar is what you need to fuel the system, no sugar highs and lows as your always low on fuel) and that's your 15 minutes. 4 hours and 45 minutes to get ten more miles. ... I did everything I could to get to 40, not a riveting total but from a tough day that would do. I ended the day on 39.7nm, only .3nm short but felt like a million miles. [3]

As you can see, Beeden used his daily goals to spur him on in the midst of great odds. He broke his 7000-mile objective into bite-sized chunks. Day by day he would seek to accomplish a small goal. Some days he achieved his goal, some days he failed.

We are all familiar with setting goals. Many churches, in their vision statements and mission statements have specific or implied goals they are shooting for. However, herein lies a subtle but dangerous trap that I want to expose.

When church planters or missionaries begin their ministry, they quite naturally have ambitions and expectations. This may involve goals and targets for church size, number and types of ministries, expectations for reaching the lost, discipling believers, and so on. If you have graduated from seminary or bible college, and have taken up a post at an existing church, others will have expectations of you as well. These can be helpful if used properly, but they also can sow seeds of anxiety, stress, and failure. When these goals are your focus, they can become heavy burdens of performance and expectation leading to many negative consequences — unmet expectations, self-condemnation, fear, rejection, self-pity, and pressure. When left unchecked, this can too often lead to burnout, despair, and quitting.

Notice the difference between this type of scenario and the apostle Paul's vision of finishing his race with joy and the ministry he had been given by Jesus — to preach the gospel of grace. Short and medium term visions and goals are fine for many purposes but they must be subservient to the superior goal of finishing your race with joy. The visions and goals discussed most often by churches and church leaders should be inferior to the ultimate goal. When secondary goals become primary goals, you are an easy target for the devil's goal — defeating you.

For many church planters, leaders and Christians alike, trials and tribulations are too often seen as opposition to a misplaced view of success. Life becomes a yoyo based on circumstances. This is an open door to striving, works of the flesh, legalism, fear of failure — all killers of joy.

When secondary goals become foremost in your life and the measure of your success, you may very well become a casualty in your ministry and personal calling. Consider matters like this. Did God call you to grow your church from 100 to 250, or from 500 to 1000? Did God call you to develop the best children's ministry in town? Or, did God call you to finish your race with joy? When your measure of success is based on short-term measurable results, the pressure of ministry may lead to the downward spiral we've discussed. This is a formula for quitting before the finish line. The fallout for you, your family, and others can be huge.

If you find yourself in this situation it is a sure sign that something is amiss at a deep level. The problem is not the results. It is not even burnout and discouragement. It is some combination of being driven by an inferior vision and believing and living a false gospel, a gospel based upon performance.

Performance and Expectation

This expression, *performance and expectation*, needs to be explored in more depth here. The Lord spoke these two words to me many years ago and it began a gradual understanding of what was operating in my life and ministry. Perhaps it has found a place in yours as well.

In looking at Paul's life we see a man fueled by passion and energized by the vision and calling he was given by Jesus on the Damascus Road. Like most faithful servants of God, he worked very hard, being a tent maker by day and a minister by night. He preached and taught late into the night, so late that one time a young man fell asleep and died falling from a window (Acts 20:7-12). He had many sleepless nights and was burdened for the churches he planted. This, however, never wore him out. There are no signs in Scripture that the pressures were defeating him. Paul ended his ministry in a Roman prison, writing his second letter to Timothy, the same passionate Paul who began his ministry years earlier. Paul ended the way he started — full of excitement and passion. He ended his race with joy.

Contrast this with the experiences of many Christian workers. So many start out excited, full of energy and passion for the ministry. Over time something happens and a decline sets in as they labor under a heavy yoke, all the while working to please God. What has happened? This question is like a broad river with many contributing tributaries, but let's quickly address a core issue. We will expand this in the next two chapters.

Expectations often lead to a performance-driven mentality. Performance is not the gospel. Performance is a perversion of the gospel of grace. We start out well, full of grace and the Spirit, but somewhere along the line performance becomes a way of life. In Galatians 3:3 Paul says, "Are you so foolish? Having begun in the Spirit, are you now being made perfect by the flesh?" The Galatians started well but something happened. It is often very subtle. It may be gradual and undetectable at first, but as sure as night follows day it leads to laboring under a heavy yoke. This yoke is constructed with elements of legalism, even though we teach a gospel of grace. Paul told the Galatians, "A little leaven leavens the whole lump" (Gal. 5:9).

It is possible, even probable, that multitudes today do not even start out well. Let me explain from my own life. I was radically saved and filled with the Holy Spirit when I was 21 years old. I lived what would be considered a normal Christian life. I had ups and downs of course, served in church, and lived as best I could. Looking back now I can see that I never truly had a personal revelation of my spiritual riches in Christ and the wonders of the glorious gospel. It has taken me years to develop my understanding of the love of God as Father, living a life fully based on grace, understanding the power of Christ in me, and enjoying the daily fellowship with the Holy Spirit.

Like so many I had a heritage of performance — to earn love and approval, to excel academically, and to achieve success in the business world. It became part of my character and personality. This drove me and it carried over into my Christian life. This was not Kingdom living and had to be changed. The Lord used the trials of ministry to open my eyes and change my life.

These two ideas (performance and expectation) work together powerfully to sow seeds of destruction into the fabric of many Christian lives and ministries. These are two important aspects in Satan's playbook. Many ministers of the gospel have fallen under the bewitching (Gal. 3:1) guile of the enemy.

This leads me to a personal story, which I will share in closing this chapter: a story of such unlikelihood that I classify it as a miracle. It is one of the altars in my life that I described earlier. The story unfolded on the Metro (subway) in Paris during a discouraging season in my ministry. For our anniversary, my wife and I decided to treat ourselves to a day in Paris. It was possible to take a 6:00 am train from London Waterloo and arrive in Paris Gare du Nord by late morning. We spent the day in Paris visiting familiar places and enjoying a tasty Parisian lunch, before catching a late train back to London.

Towards the end of the afternoon we were seated on the Metro and noticed three American couples just across from us. From their conversation it was obvious they were Christian leaders visiting Paris.

Suddenly there was one of those special moments only God could have set up. One of the men asked the other, "Brother, if God asked you to leave your life in the U.S. and come to Europe to plant a church, would you do it?" We were stunned by such a question. The moment was suddenly charged with spiritual significance. This is exactly what God had asked us to do years earlier in this same city. "What would his answer be?" we wondered silently. After a short pause, the man answered, "No, I could never do that. All my friends and colleagues from seminary are pastoring churches of at least five thousand. I could never do that." At that moment the train stopped at our station and we stepped out. We knew this was a God-moment.

Wow! What are the chances of us being on the same train, the same car, on the same day and the same minute with this tourist group in Paris? What are the odds of this question being asked soliciting this exact answer? God performed a miracle before our eyes — a miracle of personal encouragement — telling us how pleased he was with our obedience to his calling. I may have been discouraged at the time by circumstances and an inferior vision, but my Father was not. He was rejoicing over us while I was wallowing in self-pity and unfulfilled expectations.

You see, these men (myself included, for a season) were caught up in a system of performance and expectations — their own and their peers. This drove them. These expectations defined their success or failure. This is responsible for so many leaders living under such pressure that they burn themselves out and quit the ministry. The statistics are there for all to see.

Paul's lofty vision statement is like medicine to the soul; like a drink of fresh water to a thirsty traveler. It lifts the servant of God above the daily pressures to perform and sets his sights on the end game. It opens the door of his heart to the river of God, welcoming in the provisions and power of the gospel of grace.

One last look at Paul's vision statement: "But none of these things move me; nor do I count my life dear to myself, so that I may finish my race with joy, and the ministry which I received from the Lord Jesus, to testify to the gospel of the grace of God" (Acts 20:24).

His vision is a powerful example to all of us. It is a vision fit and tailored to every believer, every church planter, and every leader in the body of Christ. It is inspiring, empowering, clear, and memorable. It is short and sweet and easily committed to memory. I encourage you to memorize it and adopt it. It will be like a river of water in a dry and thirsty land.

Questions to Consider:

1. Do you have a personal vision statement? If so, how is it working out? Has it become part of your life in a meaningful way? How does it compare with Paul's? Do you feel you can adopt Paul's vision statement to be superior to yours?

2. How would you assess your life and ministry at this point? Can you identify any joy-killers? If so, do not let another year go by without dealing with them.

3. What constitutes success? How do *you* measure it? Do you think God agrees with you? What does success mean in the Kingdom of God? Was Jesus successful? Paul? Think through the parable of talents (Matthew 25:14-30) and the parable of the laborers (Matthew 20:16).

4. Is there any work of the cross yet to be done in your life? Are there areas of your life that have not been surrendered to the Lord? Are you still trying to control things?

5. Take inventory of your life — how does your life reflect on God as your father? Would you say your life is characterized more by joy or by a spirit of heaviness?

6. Has this chapter given you any fresh ideas to consider?

7. Can you agree with Paul, that no trials of life will deter you from finishing your race with joy and the ministry you have been given?

8. Take time to do an inventory of your life and ministry at this point. In light of Hebrews 12:1-2, are there any weights or sins that you are running your race with? Maybe today is the day to repent and cast them off.

CHAPTER 4

A Personal Revelation

We now turn to the third key ingredient in Paul's amazing ministry as an apostle, missionary, and church planter. All five of the components we will look at in Paul's life are essential. Similar to the ingredients in a wonderful cooking recipe, it takes all of them working together to create a winning dish. If even one is left out, the recipe is not the same.

Having said that, this matter of Paul's personal revelation of the gospel of grace is the *keystone* that holds everything else together. A *keystone* is the wedge-shaped stone at the top of an arch that locks all the stones together into a solid whole. Without the keystone the arch is weak and unstable. It cannot carry the weight and load that it was designed to carry.

This is at the heart of Paul's calling. His vision statement in Acts 20:24 summarizes the call on his life: "But none of these things move me; nor do I count my life dear to myself, so that I may finish my race with joy, and the ministry which I received from the Lord Jesus, *to testify to the gospel of the grace of God*" (emphasis mine).

This should not surprise any reader of this book. Each of us, we think, is well versed in the gospel of grace. Grace is at the heart of the good news of the gospel — we are saved by grace, saved by the finished work of Christ on the cross. He took upon himself our sins and gave to us his righteousness (2 Cor. 5:21). Our salvation is a free gift, given to us by grace, which we receive by faith (Eph. 2:8).

In a sense, you might ask, "Why is this so important? Paul knew this and we know it. Why is this a major ingredient in closing the gap between the great promises in the Word of God and the burnout and failure of so many church leaders and Christians?" There are two significant matters that we must discuss here that are all too often missing for many Christians. These are essential if the glorious gospel of grace is to be effective and powerful in our lives, as it was for Paul.

First, the gospel of grace is far more extensive and powerful than most of us realize, certainly more than many of us have experienced. When the full breadth and depth of this is understood *and experienced,* total transformation can and will take place in our lives. We will discuss this in the next chapter.

Secondly, the gospel of grace must be received by personal revelation in order to be effective in our lives. This matter of revelation is not often taught nor understood well. There is a significant difference between knowing a doctrine intellectually and having the truth of it affect our hearts in a life-changing way. Before we move into the details of what the glorious gospel of grace is, we need to explore this matter of personal revelation.

The need for personal revelation is embedded in the New Testament but overlooked by most people. Many of the most fundamental truths of our faith lie dormant and ineffectual in our minds. They remain *impotent* because they have not been energized by personal revelation. The Holy Spirit is able to light them up and drop them into your heart, in a fresh empowering way.

This has huge ramifications for your Christian life. It can be the difference between a Christian life of mediocrity and lukewarmness and a life of vibrant passion for God; the difference between a life of bondage and a life of freedom and liberty; the difference between defeat and victory; the difference between striving and a life of rest and peace; and the difference between not making it to the finish line and finishing your race with joy.

Easton's Bible Dictionary defines *revelation* (Gr. apokalupsis) as, "An uncovering, a bringing to light of that which had been previously wholly hidden or only obscurely seen." [1]

Rick Renner, a Greek scholar, describes this word *apokalupsis*, as follows:

The word "revelation" refers to something that has been veiled or hidden for a long time and then suddenly, almost instantaneously, becomes clear and visible to the mind or eye. It is like pulling the curtains out of the way so you can see what has always been just outside your window. The scene was always there for you to enjoy, but the curtains blocked your ability to see the real picture. But when the curtains are drawn apart, you can suddenly see what has been hidden from your view. The moment you see beyond the curtain for the first time and observe what has been there all along but not evident to you — that is what the Bible calls a "revelation".[2]

The apostle Paul tells us in Galatians 1:11-12 that the gospel of grace was given to him by revelation: "But I make known to you, brethren, that the gospel which was preached by me is not according to man. For I neither received it from man, nor was I taught it, but it came through the *revelation of Jesus Christ*" (emphasis mine).

Paul also described the gospel as a *mystery* (Col. 1:24-26, Eph. 6:19). The New Testament uses the word *mystery* 26 times. The Spirit Filled Life Bible describes this word in New Testament terms as a word that "denotes something that people could never know by their own understanding and that demands a revelation from God."[3]

Paul brings these ideas of mystery and revelation together in Ephesians 3:1-4. "For this reason I, Paul, the prisoner of Christ Jesus for you Gentiles— if indeed you have heard of the dispensation of the grace of God which was given to me for you, how that *by revelation* He made known to me *the mystery* (as I have briefly written already, by which, when you read, you may understand my knowledge in the mystery of Christ)," (emphasis mine).

It is very important to understand that this topic of revelation does not stop with Paul receiving the gospel from Jesus. Paul goes on to pray that his readers will also receive revelation of the truth that he is teaching and writing about. Jesus revealed it to Paul and he received it by revelation into his heart (understanding). The next step is that you and I receive it by revelation into our hearts (understanding). We see this clearly in Paul's prayer in Ephesians 1:15-23.

> Therefore I also, after I heard of your faith in the Lord Jesus and your love for all the saints, do not cease to give thanks for you, making mention of you in my prayers: that the God of our Lord Jesus Christ, the Father of glory, *may give to you the spirit of wisdom and revelation in the knowledge of Him, the eyes of your understanding being enlightened*; that you may know what is the hope of His calling, what are the riches of the glory of His inheritance in the saints, and what is the exceeding greatness of His power toward us who believe, according to the working of His mighty power which He worked in Christ when He raised Him from the dead and seated Him at His right hand in the heavenly places, far above all principality and power and might and dominion, and every name that is named, not only in this age but also in that which is to come. And He put all things under His feet, and gave Him to be head over all things to the church, which is His body, the fullness of Him who fills all in all (emphasis mine).

The word *understanding* in verse 18 is the Greek word *kardias* (Strong's 2588). Most versions translate this word as *heart*. The implication is apparent — true and deep understanding comes at a heart level whereas knowledge is a matter of the mind. Understanding vs. knowledge and heart vs. head. Understanding is superior to knowledge in that it leads us to a deeper comprehension of God himself (knowing him), not just knowing about him.

Scripture tells us what is in our heart will determine how our Christian life goes: "Out of the heart flow the issues of life" (Prov. 4:23). This is why revelation is critical for every believer, especially the church planter and church leader. Everything turns on the amount of revelation you have at a heart level.

Speaking for myself, I've had knowledge of the great doctrines of the bible. I have learned them over my nearly 50 years of being a Christian and have had the pleasure of teaching them for years. This, however, is no assurance of having a personal, life-changing revelation of them. Something dramatic happens when the Holy Spirit opens the eyes of our understanding (heart) to some of the great gospel truths. This is what happened to Martin Luther when he had a revelation of salvation by faith alone.

The Holy Spirit is the administrator of our inheritances in Christ. [4] John 16:13 says, "However, when He, the Spirit of truth, has come, He will guide you into all truth; for He will not speak on His own authority, but whatever He hears He will speak; and He will tell you things to come."

In John 6:63, Jesus tell us, "It is the Spirit who gives life; the flesh profits nothing. The words that I speak to you are spirit, and they are life." You see, the gospel Jesus taught Paul was spirit and life. Paul wrote the words, inspired by the Holy Spirit. Subsequently you and I read them in our bibles. This is where we need the Holy Spirit to open the eyes of our understanding (heart) to receive them in a life transforming way — from the Holy Spirit, to our spirits. This is what I mean by *revelation*.

Let me illustrate by giving a personal example that I shared in my booklet, *Revelation — Key To Personal Revival.*

We often need a personal revelation to fully grasp a scriptural truth. By revelation I mean an uncovering, an unveiling, a disclosure or revelation of a truth that we previously did not fully comprehend. Oh, what a glorious truth this is. What a glorious concept we now have before us. This brings hope and excitement to many a dull heart.

I remember the day when I received a personal revelation of the doctrine of justification. My life was changed forever. I came alive where I was once dead, yet I had been a Christian for over twenty years when this happened. I had been taught about justification from Romans 3, 4, and 5 and I'm sure I had heard many a sermon on the subject.

It was not, however, until that glorious day when it burst into my heart and became personal revelation, that my life was transformed forever. Here is the way it happened.

I walked into the classroom one evening and I saw what my bible college professor had written on the board in huge letters:

Righteous 24/7

I was stunned. It lit up for me. It jumped off the board and into my heart. I was receiving revelation.

That kicked off a period of weeks when I fervently read and studied everything I could get my hands on to illuminate this precious doctrine more fully. As I said, I was changed forever. I "got it." My relationship with God was deeper and more intimate than I had known before. I knew a joy, a peace and a rest that was fresh and new. Gone forever was the striving to please God that had characterized much of my Christian walk. Weariness was turned into rest.

Sometimes a personal revelation seems to come out of nowhere, a sudden quickening by the Holy Spirit. Other times it comes through diligent study of the Word of God. As in so many areas of ministry and discipleship, it is both the Word and the Spirit working together in harmony.

The devotional classic, *Streams In The Desert*, has a wonderful little discussion of this from a slightly different angle. Commenting on Luke 5:4, "When He had stopped speaking, He said to Simon, 'Launch out into the deep and let down your nets for a catch.'"

> How deep He does not say. The depth into which we launch will depend upon how perfectly we have given up the shore, and the greatness of our need, and the apprehension of our possibilities. The fish were to be found in the deep, not in the shallow water.
>
> So with us; our needs are to be met in the deep things of God. We are to launch out into the deep of God's Word, which the Spirit can open up to us in such crystal fathomless meaning that the same words we have accepted in times past will have an ocean of meaning in them, which renders their first meaning to us very shallow.
>
> Into the deep of the Atonement, until Christ's precious blood is so illuminated by the Spirit that it becomes an omnipotent balm, and food and medicine for the soul and body.
>
> Into the deep of the Father's will, until we apprehend it in its infinite minuteness and goodness, and its far-sweeping provision and care for us.

Into the deep of the Holy Spirit, until He becomes a bright, dazzling, sweet, fathomless summer sea, in which we bathe and bask and breathe, and lose ourselves and our sorrows in the calmness and peace of His everlasting presence.

Into the deep of the Holy Spirit, until He becomes a bright, marvelous answer to prayer, the most careful and tender guidance, the most thoughtful anticipation of our needs, the most accurate and supernatural shaping of our events.

Into the deep of God's purposes and coming kingdom, until the Lord's coming and His millennial reign are opened up to us; and beyond these the bright entrancing ages on ages unfold themselves, until the mental eye is dazed with light, and the heart flutters with inexpressible anticipations of its joy with Jesus and the glory to be revealed.

Into all these things, Jesus bids us launch. He made us and He made the deep, and to its fathomless depths He has fitted our longings and capabilities. [5]

As I have experienced in my own life, I would expect the same is true of many church leaders and believers — a deep, personal revelation of familiar themes in Scripture will set you on a new trajectory of life and ministry. You may think your problems and challenges in the ministry arise from such things as too much to do and too little time, too many pressures, too little money, an unappreciative church board, betrayal by a close associate, a children's ministry leader that just let you down, or expected church growth that is not happening. While these may be real, their removal as trials may not be what is needed. When the eyes of your understanding are enlightened, when the Holy Spirit takes the Word of God and brings it to life in a fresh and powerful way, we become men and women of God empowered by him to finish our race with joy in and through every trial; in a word, "overcomer." The trial itself is probably not the problem, but our response to it.

Personal Revival

I have read numerous books and accounts of revival. In 2005 my wife and I were on vacation in Scotland on the Isle of Skye. We realized we were only a short ferry ride away from the Isle of Lewis, the scene of the 1949 – 1953 revival led by Duncan Campbell. On the spur of the moment we embarked on a one-day adventure to the scene of what has become known as the Hebrides Revival or the Lewis Awakening.

One encounter led to another and we found ourselves having tea and cookies in the living room of Donald John Smith, one of the few remaining survivors of that awesome move of God. That was a day to remember as this man shared story after story of those amazing days. He seemed to still have the afterglow of that powerful move of the Holy Spirit. What a privilege to hear an eyewitness account of a sovereign move of God that transformed communities and changed thousands of lives.

One of my favorite little books about revival is "Cure Of All Ills" by Mary Stewart Relfe, Ph.D. [6] The author chronicles a history of the great American revivals. The title of her book makes the point of what I want to say here – a powerful move of God is the cure of all ills, on both a national and a personal level.

The good news is this. You do not have to wait for the rare national or regional revival. You can have it now, a personal revival. Personal revival is often the result of receiving personal revelation. When the Spirit opens your heart to receive revelation of some aspect of the glorious gospel your life is transformed and set afire with love and passion.

We see this happening to two of Jesus' disciples on the Emmaus road. The story is found in Luke 14. Verse 16 says that the disciples' eyes were restrained from recognizing their walking companion. Subsequently Jesus expanded the Scriptures concerning himself from Moses and all the Prophets. Verses 31 and 32 tell the exciting result of this revelation: "Then their eyes were opened and they knew Him; and He vanished from their sight ... Did not our heart burn within us while He talked with us on the road, and while He opened the Scriptures to us?" Their hearts were burning within them. This is personal revelation. The Holy Spirit is continuing this ministry today. Praise the Lord.

If we can say anything about Paul it is that he was a man of power — God's power working both in him and through him to others; an inward working of the resurrection power of Christ and an outward working through miraculous signs and wonders. The key to his power was his personal revelation of the full, glorious gospel. The power of the gospel is released when each facet of it becomes real in our lives. The doctrines of the gospel burst on to the scene when they break forth from knowledge to understanding, and from understanding to faith and action. They break loose from the chambers of debate in scholarly institutions on to the battlefield of the mission field, where the Kingdom of God is breaking forth against the Kingdom of darkness. Let the adventure continue.

Questions to Consider:

1. Is this idea of personal revelation new to you?
2. Can you recall in your past when you have received a deeper understanding of a biblical truth? How did it affect your Christian life?
3. Can you identify two or three truths or doctrines where you strongly desire to go deeper with God? If so, pray now and ask the Holy Spirit to teach you and reveal to you deeper truths at a heart level.
4. Try to assess your Christian walk to identify your major weakness. According to Scripture, what is God's remedy for this? Seek him for a greater revelation in this area, so that your weakness will become a strength.
5. How is your relationship with the Holy Spirit? Is he able to teach you the truths of the Scripture in a deeper way?
6. Take time to see the power Paul demonstrated in and through his teaching, life, and ministry. See Acts 19, Romans 15:18-19, 1 Corinthians 2:4-5, 2 Corinthians 12:9, Ephesians 1:19, 3:16, 19-20, and Philippians 3:10. Do you have faith to believe this can be true of your life as well?

CHAPTER 5

A Glorious Gospel

aul's revelation of the gospel is at the heart of his
successful ministry. The power of the gospel operating in his life is like the steam engine in an old train giving
it the power to climb the steep hills. In our five keys to Paul's
success I believe this is the keystone. The *power of the gospel*
working in and through Paul enabled him to overcome every
trial and every attack of Satan and finish his race with joy and
the ministry he had been given by Jesus, to preach the gospel
of grace.

The Millennium Star diamond is perhaps the most
beautiful diamond in the world. It is pear shaped, about the
size of an egg. It is the second largest D-flawless diamond
weighing in at a hefty 203.04 carats. It was cut and fashioned
into 54 facets of perfect proportions and declared to be inter-
nally and externally flawless. The greatest team of diamond
cutters in the world worked around the clock for three years
cutting and polishing this beauty.

I see the Millennium Star as a picture of the glorious gospel of grace as revealed to Paul by the Lord Jesus. It truly is a most glorious gospel — one gospel, yet numerous facets all fashioned perfectly, shined and polished to reflect light from deep within the jewel. As you shine a light while turning the diamond, rays of beautiful light flash in all directions. The diamond of the gospel of Christ sparkles like no other.

Paul's use of the word *enriched* in 1 Corinthians 1:4-6 highlights the spiritual riches every believer has in Christ. "I thank my God always concerning you for the grace of God which was given to you by Christ Jesus, that you were *enriched in everything* by Him in all utterance and all knowledge, even as the testimony of Christ was confirmed in you" (emphasis mine).

Greek scholar Rick Renner describes the meaning of the Greek word translated *enriched*. "The word 'enriched' is the Greek word *plousios*, which describes *extreme or vast material wealth*. In fact, the word *plousios* is where we get the term "plutocrat," referring to a person who is so prosperous that he is unable to ascertain the full extent of his own wealth." [1]

It is impossible, in a short book like this, to describe these great riches in depth or, using my illustration, to capture the light of every facet of the diamond. Even though a full systematic treatment of the glorious gospel is beyond the scope of this book it will be fruitful to take two approaches for the benefit of all church planters, church leaders, and believers. Let's shine a light on these two aspects of the gospel in order to observe the brilliant reflection caused by the perfectly cut facets.

These two discussions are essential understanding for every serious follower of Jesus. They hold a key in closing the gap between success and failure, between self-effort (leading to weariness and burnout) and Spirit-led ministry (resulting in joy and peace.)

Sit, Walk, Stand

This is the title of a Christian classic by Watchman Nee.[2] Nee uses these three words to capture an overview of Paul's letter to the Ephesians. Personally, I have found that a revelatory understanding of this has been life transforming. It has brought huge spiritual breakthroughs in my life and ministry. It has delivered me from a place of striving and performance to a place of rest and trust; from a place of burnout and defeat to a place of joy and victory.

Paul's letter to the Ephesians can be neatly divided into three sections.

Chapters 1-3

This section is certainly doctrinal in its teaching, but its spiritual and practical implications far exceed mere doctrine. Nee captures, from chapter 2 verse 6, the word *sit* to describe this first section of Ephesians — "... and raised us up together, and made us *sit* together in the heavenly places in Christ Jesus" (emphasis mine). Paul, in the first three chapters, shines a light on the spiritual blessings we have as sons and daughters. Nee's point in highlighting the word *sit*, is that we have been given "every spiritual blessing" (1:3) as a free gift, because of Christ's love. We don't work for them; in fact we cannot work for them. They are given to us freely.

The spiritual blessings in Ephesians 1-3 make a long list. I will lift them from the text and highlight them here so you absorb the light from each facet:

- We are chosen by Him (1:4).
- We are holy and without blame before Him in love (1:4).
- We are predestined to adoption as sons (1:5).
- We are accepted in the beloved (1:6).
- We have redemption and forgiveness of sins (1:7).
- We have received an inheritance (1:11).
- We have been sealed with the Holy Spirit, which is the guarantee of our inheritance (1:13, 14).
- We can know Him (1:17).
- We are given the exceeding greatness of his power (1:19).
- We are made alive together with Christ (2:1, 5).
- We have been raised up and seated together with Christ in heavenly places (2:6).
- His kindness has been given to us (2:7).
- Our salvation is by grace through faith, and not of works (2:8).
- We are His workmanship (2:10).
- We have been created for good works (2:10).
- We Gentiles, who were once lost, having no hope in this world, have now become one new man with believing Israel, joining them in a relationship with God. We have become part of the household of God

along with believing Israel and are fellow heirs with them (2:11-19, 3:6).

- Through Christ we now have access by one Spirit to the Father (2:18).
- Being part of this new household, we are a habitation of God in the Spirit (2:21, 22).
- We have had preached to us the unsearchable riches of Christ (3:8).
- We now have boldness and access to God through Christ (3:12).

Following this list of spiritual blessings, we come to Paul's prayer in Ephesians 3:14-21. Paul's powerful prayer adds to the spiritual gifts we can expect as part of this perfect, sparkling diamond called the gospel:

- To be strengthened with might through His Spirit in our inner man (3:16).
- Christ dwells in our hearts (3:17).
- That we may be rooted and grounded in love (3:17).
- That we are to receive personal revelation of the width and length and depth and height of Christ's love (3:18).
- That we are to comprehend (receive by personal revelation) the love of Christ, which is so great that it cannot be fully known (3:19).
- That we are to be filled with all the fullness of God (3:19).
- We are to know and experience that He can do exceedingly abundantly above all that we could ask or think because of the power that works in us (3:20).

This list in Ephesians 1-3 is by no means an exhaustive discussion of the glorious gospel. Paul says in other places such things as this: we are freely justified by faith; we are given the Holy Spirit for power, sanctification, gifts and fruit; we have fellowship with him; our hope of glory is Christ in us; the power of sin has been broken; and we have been delivered from the power of darkness.

All of these wonderful, amazing, and powerful truths are to be known, understood and received *before* we get to the second section of the letter to the Ephesians, chapters 4 and 5. We cannot strive and work for them. In fact if we try to work for them, we become like the foolish Galatians (Gal. 1:1), operating in the works of the flesh.

At the risk of repeating myself, I say once again, it is not the knowledge of these truths that is powerful, but the revelation of them personally into our lives.

Chapter 4-5

This section begins with these words, "I therefore, the prisoner of the Lord beseech you to have a walk worthy of the calling with which you were called." Paul is saying that because of all we have been freely given and because of who we *have become* as sons and daughters, we are to have a walk worthy of the Lord!

The imperative here is the order, the Godly, Kingdom order for a successful, righteous and victorious Christian life. Using the two words Nee captured from 2:6 and 3:1, we must learn to *sit before we walk*; we must rest in Christ before we begin to walk it out. To use Paul's thoughts from Philippians 2:13-14, we cannot work out our salvation until we see that he has worked it in us first. Yes, in fact we can only have a walk worthy of the Lord when we do it in the power given to us freely by grace.

This, my friend, is counterintuitive to everything we have learned and experienced in this world. It does not come naturally. From the time we are born into this world we are conditioned by life to the idea that from performance comes rewards. The world rewards performance and good deeds. Most learn this from their parents in one way or another. School teaches us that hard work produces better grades which in turn rewards us with greater opportunities and approval from parents and teachers. Most of the business world is based upon the idea of pay for performance. On the other hand, poor performance often results in reprimands, penalties, or withdrawal of love.

There is nothing inherently wrong with these systems of performance, but they are contrary to the fundamentals of God's system of love and grace. The Kingdom of God works differently than the kingdom of this world.

Understanding this contrast sheds light upon many things. Because of this, many Christians have knowledge of the gospel of grace but do not live it out in an effective way. God's extravagant love has not replaced the world's system of performance in the DNA of their lives. Their minds have not been renewed and their souls (mind, will, and emotions) have not been transformed by the truth and power of God's love. This is why Paul prayed for the Ephesians to receive *revelation* in such a way that the totality of their lives would be transformed like his was — Ephesians 1:17-19.

Why would Paul use such dramatic language as *glorious* gospel, knowing that the word gospel itself means good news? He is saying the gospel is not merely good news, but gloriously good news, spectacularly good news, awesomely good news, amazingly good news. We are able to understand his thinking in light of his personal testimony.

Paul had a total transformation from legalist to a lover of grace. He never got over this revelation. He was stunned. He sought many ways to describe it — the glorious gospel (1 Tim. 1:11), the unsearchable riches of Christ (Eph. 3:8), and Christ in you the hope of glory (Col. 1:27).

I read somewhere this definition of the gospel of grace: "God's irrational, unimaginable kindness!" It is irrational — against all earthy rationale. It is otherworldly. If Paul were with us today, I think he would agree with this definition.

This for me is something I have needed to hear over and over again. We need to be washed with this truth until it becomes part of the fabric of our lives. In the book of Jeremiah we read, speaking of the New Covenant, that God would take out our heart of stone and give to us a heart of flesh (Jer. 31:31-34 and Ez. 36:26-27). His commands become something we want to obey, not something we have to obey.

Returning to Paul's progression in Ephesians, we have a walk worthy of the Lord by living a life activated and enlivened by the power of the gospel, as the Holy Spirit reveals it to us personally. We freely live out the truths and power given to us by grace.

After understanding the divine flow of the first two sections of Ephesians, *sit* (chapters 1-3) followed by *walk* (chapters 4-5), we move to the final section, *stand.*

Chapter 6

Watchman Nee describes the third section of Ephesians with the word *stand*, from chapter 6 verses 11, 13, and 14. Again, the idea here is the order — sit before you walk and walk before you stand against the wiles of the enemy. Sit, then walk, then stand.

The Christian who deals effectively against all the schemes of the devil is the person who first is transformed by the revelation of who he or she is in Christ, (enjoying and being empowered by all the spiritual benefits of salvation) followed by a joyful, victorious, overcoming Christian walk. These are the credentials the devil hates to face. A leader who is not mature in the first two steps becomes an easy prey for the devil. He has many subtle strategies and prowls around finding the flaws in our Christian foundation, employing them strategically to bring about our downfall.

Paul's remedy is the armor of God, which he describes in Ephesians 6:10 and following. Essentially, the armor is powerful and effective when we have learned to appropriate and live out all the riches in Christ given to us freely by grace.

This progression we see in Ephesians is no a small matter. It is essential for a fruitful, healthy, and robust Christian life. We see it rooted in creation itself. God has made this concept integral to the way he relates to his created order. Allow me to digress slightly to drive home my point.

In Genesis chapters one and two we see the order in which God created everything. At the end of day six he created man, Adam and Eve, he created them male and female. Then he rested on the seventh day. This means that the first day in the life of Adam and Eve was the seventh day, the Sabbath, the day of rest. So, their week began with a day of rest. They rested before they began to work.

We see something similar in the beginning of the biblical day. Have you wondered why the biblical day begins at sunset? Seems strange. You would think the day begins at sunrise, when we get up and go to work. But no, we begin our day by sleeping before we get up and begin our work. Rest before work. Both of these examples point toward the ultimate fulfillment in what Christ has done for us in redemption. The revelation of this order in the life of a Christian will bring untold blessing; the violation will wreak havoc. Seeds of destruction are sown into the life of Christians when they get things out of proper, biblical order.

Filled With The Fullness of God

Let us now take a second approach that will shine light on other facets of this glorious diamond — Paul's gospel. It comes from Paul's prayer in Ephesians 3:19: "... to know the love of Christ which passes knowledge; *that you may be filled with all the fullness of God*" (emphasis mine).

Paul's prayer, that we are to be *filled with all the fullness of God,* seems to be beyond comprehension. I have asked myself for years, what does this fully mean? Paul received profound revelation from Jesus following his conversion on the Damascus Road. This revelation he called the glorious gospel (1 Timothy 1:11). It became the life transforming power that enabled him to overcome all trials and sufferings and finish his race with joy. Upon discovery of Paul's prayer that we may be "... filled with all the fullness of God," we need to passionately pursue the truth of this for our own lives.

Most would agree with this statement: the greatest revelation we need is of God himself — Father, Son, and Holy Spirit. Paul records this as his prayer for the believers in Ephesus in chapter 1 verse 17: "... that the God of our Lord Jesus Christ, the Father of glory, may give to you the spirit of wisdom and *revelation in the knowledge of Him*" (emphasis mine).

Peter confirms this in 2 Peter 1:2-4:

Grace and peace be multiplied to you *in the knowledge of God and of Jesus our Lord*, as His divine power has given to us all things that pertain to life and godliness, *through the knowledge of Him* who called us by glory and virtue, by which have been given to us exceedingly great and precious promises, that through these you may be partakers of the divine nature, having escaped the corruption that is in the world through lust (emphasis mine).

For the victorious and fruitful life of every believer, there are life-transforming truths available in a deeper understanding of God himself.

A.W. Tozer, in his book *The Knowledge of the Holy*, states, "What comes into your mind when you think about God is the most important thing about us. The man who comes to a right belief about God is relieved of ten thousand problems ..." [3]

Let's expand on Paul's and Peter's exhortation of knowing God in a richer and deeper way. Paul's prayer in Ephesians 3:19 astounds me in its implications — "... to know the love of Christ which passes knowledge; that you may be filled with all the fullness of God." To be filled with the fullness of God! How we need to have a greater understanding and revelation of God himself.

As a way of opening this up, let us use Paul's doxology in 2 Corinthians 13:14 as a guide. "The grace of the Lord Jesus Christ, and the love of God, and the communion of the Holy Spirit be with you all. Amen."

Here Paul speaks of the Trinity in these terms:

- The grace of the Lord Jesus Christ.
- The love of God (the Father).
- The communion (fellowship) of the Holy Spirit.

I find it helpful, in understanding the depth of Paul's prayer "... to be filled with the fullness of God," to think in these terms. Each of these three persons of the Trinity has been the subject of numerous books and the foundational inspiration of many ministries. As such, I can only give the briefest discussion of each in the context of this book. Nevertheless, many riches lie on the surface. Let's have a look.

The Grace of our Lord Jesus Christ

Every spiritual blessing we have been given is because of the work of Christ on the cross, a work of love and grace. Here I want to mention the idea of who we *have become in Christ*. This concept is a most helpful and powerful truth that, when received by revelation and appropriated by faith, will empower any believer to live a life of freedom from bondage and have a walk worthy of the Lord, finishing his or her race with joy.

Perhaps the most foundational of all is found in 2 Corinthians 5:21: "For He made Him who knew no sin to be sin for us, that we might become the righteousness of God in Him [Christ]." As part of the great exchange at the cross, Jesus took our sins upon himself and credited to us the righteousness of God. Imagine this — the righteousness of God himself. [4]

We are righteous with the righteousness of God because we are in Christ. If you are born again you are righteous 24/7. This truth alone will bring a rest to the soul of countless church leaders and believers alike. This is only the beginning of a long list of spiritual benefits we can freely receive because of the grace of our Lord Jesus Christ.

Here is a short list of additional truths that will enable and empower us to be filled with the fullness of God, as a consequence of being in Christ. There are dozens more.

- I have been adopted as God's child (Eph. 1:5).
- I have direct access to God through the Holy Spirit (Eph. 2:18).

- I have been justified (Rom. 5:1).
- I am complete in Christ (Col. 1:20).
- I am free from condemnation (Rom. 8:1).
- I am free from the power of sin (Rom. 6:6).
- I am a partaker of a heavenly calling (Heb. 3:1).
- I have been given spiritual authority (Lu. 10:19).
- I have been chosen and appointed to bear fruit (Jn. 15:16).
- I am seated with Christ in heavenly places (Eph. 2:6).
- I can do all things through Christ who strengthens me (Phil. 4:13).

As I discussed in the previous chapter, the power of these truths becomes activated in your life when the Holy Spirit opens the eyes of your understanding and these truths burst into your heart – personal revelation.

This theological truth goes even further. There is another side of this coin. Paul not only speaks of who we are *in Christ*, but Christ is *in us*. "But when it pleased God, who separated me from my mother's womb and called me through His grace, *to reveal His Son in me*, that I might preach Him among the Gentiles, I did not immediately confer with flesh and blood," (Gal. 1:15-16, emphasis mine).

I find the Christian writers of past generations caught the revelation of this powerful truth and wrote about it extensively. We need to re-capture this today for our generation. As just one sample, I will quote again from *Streams In The Desert* (September 27). The writers quoted in this classic devotional wrote and ministered in the last half of the 19th century.

Divine healing is just divine life. It is the headship of Christ over the body. It is the life of Christ in the frame. It is the union of our members with the very body of Christ and the inflowing life of Christ in our living members. It is as real as His risen and glorified body. It is as reasonable as the fact that He was raised from the dead and is a living Man with a true body and a rational soul today at God's right hand.

That living Christ belongs to us in all His attributes and powers. We are members of His body, His flesh and His bones, and if we can only believe and receive it, we may live upon the very life of the Son of God. Lord, help me to know 'the Lord for the body and the body for the Lord.'— A. B. Simpson

"The Lord thy God in the midst of thee is mighty" (Zeph. 3:17). This was the text that first flashed the truth of Divine healing into my mind and worn-out body nearly a quarter century ago. It is still the door, wide open more than ever, through which the living Christ passes moment by moment into my redeemed body, filling, energizing, vitalizing it with the presence and power of His own personality, turning my whole being into a "new heaven and new earth." "The Lord, thy God." Thy God. My God. Then all that is in God Almighty is mine and in me just as far as I am able and willing to appropriate Him and all that belongs to Him. This God, "Mighty," ALL Mighty God, is our INSIDE God. He is, as Father, Son and Holy Spirit, in the midst of me, just as really as the sun is in the center of the heavens, or like the great dynamo in the center of the power-house of my three-fold being. He is in the midst, at the center of my physical being. He is in the midst of my brain. He is in the midst of my nerve centers.

For twenty-one years it has been not only a living reality to me, but a reality growing deeper and richer, until now at the age of seventy years, I am in every sense a younger, fresher man than I was at thirty. At this present time I am in the strength of God, doing full twice as much work, mental and physical, as I have ever done in the best days of the past, and this observe, with less than half the effort then necessary. My life, physical, mental and spiritual, is like an artesian well—always full, overflowing. To speak, teach, travel by night and day in all weather and through all the sudden and violent changes of our variable climate, is no more effort to me than it is for the mill-wheel to turn when the stream is full or for the pipe to let the water run through.

> My body, soul and spirit thus redeemed,
> Sanctified and healed I give, O Lord, to Thee,
> A consecrated offering Thine ever more to be.
> That all my powers with all their might
> In Thy sole glory may unite. —Hallelujah!

—Dr. Henry Wilson [5]

I trust you are hungry for a deeper revelation available to you as you catch the reflected light of this facet of the glorious gospel — the grace of Jesus Christ. The experiences of A.B. Simpson and Dr. Henry Wilson should inspire each of us to press into and receive the truth of *Christ in us*, the hope of glory.

Now let us move on to the second member of the Trinity as Paul writes in 2 Corinthians 13:14.

The Love of the Father

Sonship. What an amazing work of love and grace for us. The thought of being a member of God's family has huge ramifications to the life of every believer. Jesus came to reveal God as Father (Jn. 17:6, 26), and told us to pray, "Our Father in heaven, hallowed be Your name" (Matt. 6:9). The great thing about our salvation is not only a Savior, but a Father as well — not just sins forgiven but a family received.

John 17:26 — "And I have declared to them Your name, [Father] and will declare it, that the love with which You loved Me may be in them, and I in them." The very love with which the Father loved the Son is in you. This is not merely theoretical love or doctrinal love, but it is in you —

felt love. Love is the strongest power on earth. It is the most healing balm for everything that ails the soul.

This love of the Father, when received by revelation, is life transforming. It is something tangible and felt. It destroys many issues Christians, including church leaders, have — insecurity, condemnation, rejection, performance, legalism, unbelief, fear and anxiety, a lack of intimacy with God, self-pity, and much more.

We see the father's love displayed in the parable of the prodigal son in Luke 15:11-32. We see the father looking with expectancy for his son's return. Then, as he sees him afar off, he runs toward him and smothers him in kisses. In verse 21 we see the son protesting, but his father would not hear it. His love for his son would not be quenched or held back because of his son's past sins and feelings of unworthiness. Notice also what the father says to his older son in verse 31, "Son, all that I have is yours."

"All that I have is yours." Allow yourself to contemplate the depth of that for a minute. It is as if Father is saying to you and me, "You are my son; as with Jesus so with you — my love, my approval, my leading, freedom, joy, strength, authority, the hearing of my voice, grace for every situation, supply for all your needs, fellowship with my Spirit, seated alongside my son Jesus in heavenly places, and your future inheritance insured — a free gift from me, your Father."

Having pastored in Great Britain for 19 years, I find the comparison with being a member of the royal family helpful in grasping this truth. Every British citizen is a subject of the Queen of England. She is their Queen and they live in her kingdom, the United Kingdom. Most citizens admire and love her. They benefit in many ways from her reign. However, they would find it nearly impossible to have a private meeting with her. They do not know her personally and the Queen does not know them by name or in any meaningful way. She is known only from a distance.

Compare this with her three sons, her daughter, and her grandchildren. They know her personally and have open access to her. They eat with her, talk with her, celebrate with her and are personally loved by her. They are not so much her subjects, but her family. They receive all the benefits of *being a royal* — prestige, honor, power, responsibility, and inheritance. The Queen loves each of them because they came from her. They are hers.

This latter idea was instrumental in my personal journey of revelation of God as my father, dad, and Abba (Hebrew). My father died when I was a young boy. I was adopted but never felt truly loved by my adopted father. As a consequence, I struggled for much of my Christian life receiving God's father-love into my heart. Although I was not conscious of it at the time, I have now come to see that my relationship with God was contaminated with a performance attitude. I was not rooted and grounded in his unconditional love for me.

It all began to change one day as I observed my heart for my own children and grandchildren. As a father and grandfather, I began to see that I loved my children and grandchildren, not because of what they do, but because of who they are. *They are mine.* Even if my own children were not as smart, or hadn't the same level of achievements as yours, I could still never love your child as much as my own, for one reason — *they are mine!*

My love for them has nothing to do with their performance or their earning my love. They are my flesh and blood. My love springs from this family relationship — a love so deep it is unconditional and unbreakable. They receive all the privileges of being in my family. They are my beneficiaries and will receive all that I can possibly bestow upon them.

Now extend this to our Father in heaven. Paul brings this truth to us with a real punch in Galatians 4:6-7. "And because you are sons, God has sent forth the Spirit of His Son into your hearts, crying out, 'Abba, Father!' Therefore you are no longer a slave but a son, and if a son, then an heir of God through Christ." In Chapter 2 we talked about being certain of your calling. In order to imitate Paul I encouraged you to be certain of your calling. However, after being born again, our number one calling is it to be a son or daughter. He has adopted you and brought you into his family. He has put his Spirit in you, the Spirit of sonship. The deepest cry of your heart should be *Abba, Father.*

You have a place of intimacy with him that is not based upon your performance or what you do for him. You enjoy full access to him and to his heart because you are his. You are secure in his love knowing he enjoys you for who you are. There is nothing you can do to make him love you more. Your good works add nothing to his love for you. Rest in this wonderful truth. Allow it to soak into your heart and change your life and ministry.

The Fellowship of the Holy Spirit

Now we move to the third member of the Trinity, that Paul describes as the "fellowship [Greek, koinonia] of the Holy Spirit" in 2 Corinthians 13:14. Let me ask you this question. What is your relationship with the Holy Spirit? Are you close to him? Do you have fellowship with him?

A.W. Tozer, in chapter 5 of his Christian classic, *God's Pursuit of Man*, describes the Holy Spirit as the *Forgotten One.* [6] Tozer observes that much of the body of Christ has the Holy Spirit in its doctrine, but little in its services and presumably, in their personal lives. Is he the forgotten one in your walk with God? He was at the heart of Paul's life and ministry.

When Jesus was about to be crucified he told his disciples that it was to their advantage that he leave, because he would send them the Holy Spirit, whom he called the Helper (Jn. 16:7). How many of us would agree that it is to our advantage to have the Holy Spirit here with us and in us, compared to Jesus in the flesh?

The Holy Spirit comforts us (Acts 9:31), teaches us (Jn. 14:26), guides us into all truth and tells us things to come (Jn. 16:13), dwells with us (Jn. 14:17), empowers us to carry on the ministry of Jesus (Jn. 14:12, Acts 1:8), seals our salvation and guarantees our inheritance (Eph. 1:13-14), helps our weaknesses (Rom. 8:26), sanctifies us (Rom. 15:16), gives us joy (Rom. 14:17), bears fruit in our lives (Gal. 5:22-23), and gives us gifts (1 Cor. 12:3-11).

Jesus was anointed by the Holy Spirit at his baptism (Matt. 3:16), performed miracles by the Holy Spirit (Matt. 12:28), was filled with the Holy Spirit (Lu. 4:1), and was raised from the dead by the Holy Spirit (Rom. 1:4). We see the same pattern in the disciples following their baptism of the Holy Spirit in Acts 2:1-4. If Jesus needed the Holy Spirit and the disciples needed him as well, how much more do we need him today?

Koinonia has a "whole flavor of meanings, but one primary meaning is *partnership*."[7] As pastors and leaders, we often feel alone in the ministry. The Holy Spirit wants to be your partner in ministry. We see this in Jesus' life and in Paul's life; why not yours? You are not alone in your calling, whether you lead a church, run a business, or raise a family. This is part of the glorious gospel of grace.

Above I mentioned a few of the benefits and works of the Holy Spirit in us. However, it is not so much what he does, but who he is. The Holy Spirit loves you deeply. You have the wonderful privilege of cultivating an intimate, personal relationship with the Holy Spirit. He knows you personally. Your attitude towards the Spirit of God is critical. Do you love him? Is your life and your body a pleasant place for him to inhabit and enjoy? Do you do everything possible to deepen your knowledge of him and your relationship with him? Does he have preeminence in your life? Fellowship with the Holy Spirit is essential for a God-infused, power-filled life and ministry.

James jolts us with the importance of this in chapter 4, verses 4-5, "Adulterers and adulteresses! Do you not know that friendship with the world is enmity with God? Whoever therefore wants to be a friend of the world makes himself an enemy of God. Or do you think that the Scripture says in vain, *'The Spirit who dwells in us yearns jealously'"* (emphasis mine)?

"The Spirit who dwells in us yearns jealously." The Greek word translated *yearns* is *epipotheo*. This is a word that portrays "an intense desire; a craving; a hunger; an ache; a yearning for something; a longing or pining for something." [8] The Spirit of God has a deep love for each of us. He is jealous of us in the sense that he does not want any other thing to replace him in our hearts. He wants no rivals. He has been called the Divine Lover. He wants your love, attention, fellowship, and communion. He wants time alone with you. He desires intimacy. In turn he will give you everything you need to live this life and finish your race with joy. Remember what Jesus said in John 7:37-39:

> On the last day, that great day of the feast, Jesus stood and cried out, saying, "If anyone thirsts, let him come to Me and drink. He who believes in Me, as the Scripture has said, out of his heart will flow rivers of living water." But this He spoke concerning the Spirit, whom those believing in Him would receive; for the Holy Spirit was not yet *given,* because Jesus was not yet glorified.

The times in which we live are busy and exhausting. Most church leaders and believers alike find themselves consumed with duties and tasks. They are worn out. Jesus promises that the Holy Spirit will be like a refreshing river of water, quenching every thirst you have. This was key to Paul's success. He drank daily. In 2 Corinthians 4:16 Paul says, "Therefore we do not lose heart. Even though our outward man is perishing, yet the inward man is being renewed day by day."

Prospective church planter, church leader, and every follower of Jesus, in this chapter I have uncovered for you two sources of spiritual life itself — two of the keys to living a victorious, overcoming, and fruitful Christian life and ministry.

- Enjoy the rest of sitting before you walk and stand.
- Receive the fullness of God — the grace of Jesus Christ, the love of the Father, and the fellowship of the Holy Spirit.

Your greatest need is to know God more and more. *Your greatest source of everything you need in life and ministry is God himself.* Methods and models may bring a measure of success for a time, but to finish your race with joy and deliver to Jesus all the fruit he deserves, you need God himself on a daily basis — not just Jesus as savior, but God — Father, Son, and Holy Spirit.

Many leaders will identify with King David's defeat at Ziklag. You will find this story in 1 Samuel 30. Upon returning to this city, David and his men found it burned and all their families taken captive by the Amalekites. As you can imagine, David was "greatly distressed, and the people spoke of stoning him" (1 Sam. 30:6). Many church leaders know how David might have felt! He was obeying God, fighting the enemies of Israel, and composing songs along the way. Suddenly he has suffered a defeat and his men wanted to stone him. A familiar story for many!

In this great crisis, what did David do? "David strengthened himself in the Lord his God" (verse 6). God himself was David's source of strength. The New Testament gives us much more revelation about God than David could have known, including the grace of Jesus Christ, the love of the Father, and the fellowship of the Holy Spirit. May each of us find everything we need in God himself.

In closing this chapter let me return to the Millennial Star diamond as an illustration of the gospel. The greatest diamond cutters in the world studied this diamond extensively before they decided to fashion 54 facets. Before the diamond was cut its beauty was unseen, locked inside. It looked pretty much like any rock from the outside. Its beauty needed to be released by cutting and polishing each facet by master diamond cutters.

The gospel is similar. To many, the gospel becomes so familiar it is little more than an ordinary rock — its amazing beauty has not been unlocked to reveal the glorious light. As you receive personal revelation of a facet of the gospel, it is as if you cut one of those facets to reveal the glory inside. The more facets you know by revelation and experience personally, the greater its beauty.

Paul's Prayer

The Apostle's wonderful prayer in Ephesians 1 is for you personally:

> Therefore I also, after I heard of your faith in the Lord Jesus and your love for all the saints, do not cease to give thanks for you, making mention of you in my prayers: that

the God of our Lord Jesus Christ, the Father of glory, may give to you the *spirit of wisdom and revelation in the knowledge of Him, the eyes of your understanding being enlightened*; that you may know what is the hope of His calling, what are the riches of the glory of His inheritance in the saints, and what is the exceeding greatness of His power toward us who believe, according to the working of His mighty power (v. 15-19, emphasis mine).

I hope this chapter has enticed you to explore further the treasures of the deep — things of God found in the glorious gospel of grace. Jesus commanded his disciples to "Launch out into the deep and let down your nets for a catch" (Lu. 5:4). Jonathan Cahn gives a wonderful exhortation on this verse:

> The blessings of God aren't found in the shallow waters. You won't find them in the shallow waters of faith. They don't swim there. There are many who call themselves by Messiah's name, but most dwell only in the shallow waters. They stay by the shore. They stay near that which is familiar and comfortable. They only know the shallow waters of God. They believe, but with a shallow faith. They read the Scriptures, but only get into the shallow of the Word, the surface, the letter. And they know of God's love, but they never get into the deep of His love. As a result, they never know the deep blessings that God has for them. But if you want the blessings of God, you must leave the shallow and launch out away from the shore, away from its distractions, away from the old and the familiar, and into the deep ... into the deep waters of faith, the deep waters of His presence, the deep of His Word, the deep of worship, the deep of His joy, the deep of His voice, the deep of His Spirit, and the deep of His heart. That's where your blessings are waiting and will be found." [9]

We will now move on to the fourth key to Paul's success in reaching his goal — to finish his race with joy and the ministry he had been given by the Lord Jesus, to preach the gospel of grace.

Questions to consider:

1. How would you assess your life with respect to sit, walk, and stand? Is your life characterized by the biblical order in Ephesians — first sitting, then walking and standing?
2. Would your friends describe you as a person of rest, peace, and joy?
3. What aspect of the glorious gospel do you need personal revelation?
4. Is there a facet of the gospel described in this chapter that will bring victory and joy in your life currently? If so, why not receive it today by faith and rejoice?
5. What might it mean to your life and ministry to be filled with the fullness of God?
6. Meditate this week on Paul's three descriptions of the Trinity: the grace of Jesus, the love of the Father, and the fellowship of the Holy Spirit.
7. Do you place greater faith in your own abilities and methods or in God himself?
8. This week think about what it means to know God as Father. Do you feel you act like a son or daughter and enjoy the benefits of sonship? What is your relationship with your earthly father? Does it reflect on your relationship with your heavenly Father?
9. What is your attitude towards the Holy Spirit? Scripture warns us about grieving him with our sin (Eph. 4:30-33), resisting him (Acts 7:51), and quenching him in our meetings (1 Thess. 5:19). Do any of these describe you?

10. Look closely at Paul's prayer in Colossians 1:9-12. See how being an overcomer is contingent on being strengthened with might and power. What does this mean? Is your relationship with the Holy Spirit conducive to receiving this?

11. Where are you fishing – in the shallow waters near the shore or in the deep waters? Does anything need to change? (See Luke 5:4-11).

A Strong Finish

In 2012 I was privileged to live in Britain and fulfill one of my lifelong desires — to attend the Summer Olympics. I have always loved the Summer Olympics since I was a boy, watching the competition between Team USA and Team CCCP (the former Soviet Union). In 1968 I enjoyed watching on television as a friend of mine won the high jump in the Mexico City Olympics. In the summer of 2012, as the Olympics were drawing near, my excitement grew.

The demand for tickets was so great they were allocated by random draw. As a result, our family received tickets mostly for the Paralympic Games. My disappointment was short lived. I was brought to tears (literally) watching the Paralympic events in the Aquatics Centre and in the Olympic Stadium, before 80,000 fans. To watch and cheer athletes swim length after length of the pool missing one, two, or three limbs was life changing for me.

The most decorated athlete in all the London 2012 Olympics was twenty-year-old Australian swimmer Jacqueline Freney, who has cerebral palsy. Freney garnered 8 gold medals. Afterward she said, "I have been training really hard for about eight years now, so I really feel that it's just been my determination and passion for the sport over that time that has got me through to these gold medals." [1]

This brings us to the fourth attribute that empowered Paul the apostle to be so successful as the premier church planter of all time — ENDURANCE.

Endurance to Finish Strong

The Greek word *hupomeno* means endurance. It comes from two Greek words: *hupo*, meaning under, as to be under something, and *meno* meaning to stay or abide. It conveys the idea of being steadfast, consistent, unwavering, and unflinching ... the attitude that hangs in there, never giving up, refusing to surrender to obstacles, and turning down every opportunity to quit. The early church called *hupomeno* the "queen of all virtues" for good reason. [2]

This is the attitude we see in Paul's life when he says in his vision statement: *"But none of these things move me;* nor do I count my life dear to myself, so that I may finish my race with joy, and the ministry which I received from the Lord Jesus, to testify to the gospel of the grace of God" (Acts 20:24, emphasis mine).

No matter what Paul faced, giving up was not an option. He and the early church believers were faced with persecution and trials like few of us will ever face — they were burned at the stake, fed to hungry lions, cut in two, beheaded, and exiled to remote islands, to name just a few.

I remember reading *Foxes Book of Martyrs* many years ago. Reading the real life stories of our ancestors in the faith is a stirring experience. The trials they faced dwarf the trials we face today in the West. We have much to learn from our brothers and sisters in the past. We have much to learn from great athletes as well, who overcome every obstacle, refusing to give up.

It is interesting to note that Paul considered perseverance an apostolic gift! In 2 Corinthians 12:12 he listed this along with signs and wonders as a gift of his calling: "Truly the signs of an apostle were accomplished among you with all *perseverance*, in signs and wonders and mighty deeds." My friend, if you are a church planter you also are a "sent one," an apostle.

When Paul was running his race, he had his eye on the finish line and the rewards that awaited him. In writing from prison to the saints in Philippi he said it this way:

> Not that I have already attained, or am already perfected; but I press on, that I may lay hold of that for which Christ Jesus has also laid hold of me. Brethren, I do not count myself to have apprehended; but one thing I do, forgetting those things which are behind and reaching forward to those things which are ahead, I press toward the goal for the prize of the upward call of God in Christ Jesus (Phil. 3:12-14).

This is not dissimilar to a modern-day athlete who runs a race or competes in a game. They run the race to win. NFL football players train and play the game to win the Super Bowl. It motivates them and empowers them to endure the exhausting work in the training room, overcome the inevitable injuries and shake off every defeat. Hebrews 6:11-12 puts it this way. "And we desire that each one of you show the same diligence to the full assurance of hope until the end, that you do not become sluggish [lazy], but imitate those who through faith and patience [endurance] inherit the promises."

We live in a day, not so much of great persecution, but of saints weary from the work, stress, time pressures, and expectations placed upon them. It is easy to get worn out and become sluggish. Left unchecked, this can lead to a downward spiral, resulting in burnout and dropping out of the race.

Paul could have been speaking directly to pastors and leaders today when he said, "And let us not grow weary while doing good, for in due season we shall reap if we do not lose heart" (Gal. 6:9). Here Paul is giving us a reason to persevere. Keep on going, keep on doing good, he says, for there will be a "due season," a "*kairos* time," in which you will be rewarded.

Paul also says, "Do not lose heart," yet this is precisely what happens to so many today. Losing heart is a common theme among pastors, leaders and believers alike. The work of the ministry and life itself can be fraught with constant opposition, division, and disappointment. For many leaders ministry can seem like a roller coaster — a season of positive fruit and momentum followed by a sudden downturn or decline. Three steps forward, two steps backward. As one season of trials and problems becomes history and a little breathing room arrives, another set of troubles arrive. Life can often feel like this.

Take heart my friend; you are not alone. This is not something new. Followers of Jesus have been experiencing this for 2,000 years. Athletes also accept this as part of their mission, as they are constantly motivated to overcome their injuries, failures and losses in order to win, or attain their PB (personal best).

As Christians, we have a huge advantage over the world — the promises of the Word remain true and our destiny is certain. The glorious gospel is as powerful and real as it was 2000 years ago. We still have the indwelling Holy Spirit and the resurrected Christ. We are still called to live a life of victory and finish our race with joy. The prize we aim for will never perish. We are only passing through this world. Paul set his eyes on his destiny, not his circumstances. Paul had a revelation of heaven in his heart and that power kept him going in dark times.

I see three critical elements that we need to discuss in more detail with respect to endurance. Each of these was a powerful component in Paul's life, enabling him to finish his race with joy, and the ministry he had been given.

A Proper Motivation

Let's start at the beginning. I considered having this first component of endurance as the first chapter in this book because it is the precursor to everything else. The all-important question is this — do we serve the Lord out of love or out of duty? This question goes to the heart of our deepest motivations in living out our Christian life. Even if we start out well, full of passion and love, many gradually slide into a "works" mentality, serving out of duty. I suspect this is often an underlying cause of leaders wearing out and giving up.

Athletes, like Jacqueline Freney, are empowered by love for the sport. Her endurance was the direct result of the passion in her heart. If it is true for a swimmer, how much more for those of us who love Jesus?

In studying the life of Paul, we see the key to his life-long love. He never forgot where he came from.

> And I thank Christ Jesus our Lord who has enabled me, because He counted me faithful, putting me into the ministry, although I was formerly a blasphemer, a persecutor, and an insolent man; but I obtained mercy because I did it ignorantly in unbelief. And the grace of our Lord was exceedingly abundant, with faith and love which are in Christ Jesus. This is a faithful saying and worthy of all acceptance, that Christ Jesus came into the world to save *sinners, of whom I am chief*. However, for this reason I obtained mercy, that in me first Jesus Christ might show all longsuffering, as a pattern to those who are going to believe on Him for everlasting life. Now to the King eternal, immortal, invisible, to God who alone is wise, be honor and glory forever and ever. Amen (1 Tim. 1:12-17, emphasis mine).

Paul calls himself the chief sinner! What a statement. He never forgot from whence he came. This is key if we are to maintain our passion for God. Jesus teaches this in the powerful story of the sinful woman in Luke chapter 7. While Jesus was dining at the home of a Pharisee, a sinful woman entered the house and came up to him "... and stood at His feet behind Him weeping; and she began to wash His feet with her tears, and wiped them with the hair of her head; and she kissed His feet and anointed them with the fragrant oil" (Luke 7:38). This is a wonderful picture of passion and worship.

The Pharisee was indignant, even questioning if Jesus was a prophet. Jesus then told him a parable about two debtors. One debtor owed a small amount of money; the other had a huge debt. The creditor forgave both debts. Jesus then asked the question that put a dagger into the heart of the Pharisee's attitude, "Tell Me therefore, which of them will love him more?" I can see a slight twinkle in Jesus' eye with this gotcha question. Simon, the Pharisee, managed to cough up the only possible answer, "I suppose the one whom he forgave more."

He who is forgiven much loves much.

This same idea carries over nicely into marriage. The marriage that lasts to the end with joy is the marriage where love is not replaced with duty. Duty brings weariness, dryness, and death. Many a marriage has begun in love and somewhere along the line turned into a business partnership. This can be an unseen disease that eventually drains the life out of many marriages.

I live a few hundred yards from the Pacific Ocean. The views are beautiful and the weather is stunning. There is however, one sinister process silently underway. The salt air combines with iron to produce rust. I never knew so many things have iron in them. Rust, rust, rust. Gate locks that once were shiny, turning easily with the slightest twist of the key, become corroded, barely able to turn without breaking off the key in the lock.

This is a picture of many workers in the Kingdom of God. They start off shiny and bright, full of passion and love. Everything is oiled and well lubricated. Then, somewhere along the line, the flames of love begin to dwindle and the rust of duty sets in. It is then only a short distance to stress, weariness, and burnout.

My wife was recently recalling the story of a woman who many years ago stood up in our church. She had just lost her elderly husband and the funeral was only days past. As she stood up, most assumed she was going to thank the church for their love and support during her time of grief. To our surprise, she simply said, *Jesus Christ has many workers, but not many lovers.* Then she sat down.

Like taking one's blood pressure from time to time to make sure we are healthy, we all need to check the level of our passion and motivation. Heart disease is a silent killer; so also it is in the spiritual realm. This is something all church planters need to know for the future. It is also something every church leader would do well to assess personally. Are we ministering and serving out of love or out of duty?

A Strong Faith

To adapt an old saying, faith and patience (endurance) go together like a horse and carriage. You cannot have strong endurance without great faith. They cannot be separated. Endurance will inevitably follow a man or woman who

She came to me on a Saturday and asked, "Daddy, can we go ice skating today?" A simple request for sure. It would cost about $10 for Chrissie and her brother to go skating. I can still recall the emotion that welled up in my heart as I said something like, "Chrissie, I'm really sorry, but we just cannot afford it." As I remember I counter proposed something that would cost nothing, like going to the park!

Immediately I sensed the Holy Spirit say very clearly to my heart, "How much do you have in your pocket?" Like Jesus did when questioning the Pharisee, he put a dagger directly into the attitude of my heart. He has a way of cutting to the core of the matter. It wasn't that I didn't have $10 in my pocket; it was that my bank account was getting very low and there was little income on the horizon. I knew what my father was saying to me. *My son, there will be a flow of money that I will provide. Don't hold on to the $10 out of fear. Trust me.* So we went skating! For me personally, this was a small event with a mighty lesson. Abba was teaching his son to trust him. Thank goodness I passed that little test. Greater ones awaited me.

These greater trials soon came along. Sitting here today I could tell of miracle after miracle of God's provision. My trials may be different from yours, but we are all in the same school — the school of life. In this life you will have tribulations. Jesus said it this way in John 16:33: "These things I have spoken to you, that *in Me* you may have peace. In the world you will have tribulation; but be of good cheer, I have overcome the world" (emphasis mine).

Abraham is called the Father of Faith. Paul retells this story in Romans 4, to explain how righteousness is accounted to us by faith. When Abraham was 75 God promised him and Sarah a son. Abraham waited 25 years until the promise was fulfilled in Isaac. Despite their bodies wrinkling with age and any chance of Sarah becoming pregnant vanishing, Abraham held on in faith. Paul picks up the story when Abraham was about 100 years old. His words are a wonderful glimpse into Abe's thinking:

> And not being weak in faith, he did not consider his own body, already dead (since he was about a hundred years old), and the deadness of Sarah's womb. He did not waver at the promise of God through unbelief, but was strengthened in faith, giving glory to God, and being fully convinced that what He had promised He was also able to perform. And therefore "it was accounted to him for righteousness" (Rom. 4:19-22).

This is what God has for each of us. We are able to look beyond our circumstances, through the eyes of faith, and see God at work. Even in the midst of the difficulties of ministry we are able to give God glory, knowing with certainty our calling is from God. He will perform whatever is necessary, give every grace, and empower us to finish our race with joy.

Strong faith produces peace in your life and ministry. My fellow church planter or church leader, you are called to a ministry of peace; a peace that passes understanding, because you are *in him* and *he is in you*. A peace that exists because your faith has become strong. You are only able to live in victory and minister in peace with strong faith.

I remember a message by Pastor Jon Courson (Applegate Christian Fellowship, Jacksonville, Oregon) during our time under his ministry as he preached through Romans. This was at the outset of my own ministry in the early 90's. God knew that I would be a striver and he was teaching me early on from one of the great teachers of God's love and grace. Pastor Jon spoke from Ezekiel 44:17-18. Speaking of the Levitical priests, it says:

> And it shall be, whenever they enter the gates of the inner court, that they shall put on linen garments; no wool shall come upon them while they minister within the gates of the inner court or within the house. They shall have linen turbans on their heads and linen trousers on their bodies; *they shall not clothe themselves with anything that causes sweat* (emphasis mine).

Pastor Jon used this as a powerful picture of a no-sweat ministry! This is God's desire for each of you. Isn't this really a description of Paul's ministry? He had trials upon trials, but they became his credentials, not his destroyer. He was a man of peace; a man of great faith who endured to the end. Imitate Paul.

An indispensable aspect of Paul's faith was his hope in heaven. This hope, this confident expectation of heaven, gave him the strength and encouragement to overcome every obstacle and endure in the darkest of times. Let us recall together that Paul himself had a supernatural experience of heaven, as recorded it in 2 Corinthians 12:1-4:

> It is doubtless not profitable for me to boast. I will come to visions and revelations of the Lord: I know a man in Christ

who fourteen years ago—whether in the body I do not know, or whether out of the body I do not know, God knows—such a one was caught up to the third heaven. And I know such a man—whether in the body or out of the body I do not know, God knows— how he was caught up into Paradise and heard inexpressible words, which it is not lawful for a man to utter.

This experience would change anybody's life! Paul knew with certainty what was in store for him when his race was finished. He wrote about it often in his letters. It is worth our time to review just two of them. Colossians 3:1-3: "If then you were raised with Christ, seek those things which are above, where Christ is, sitting at the right hand of God. Set your mind on things above, not on things on the earth. For you died, and your life is hidden with Christ in God. When Christ *who is* our life appears, then you also will appear with Him in glory." Paul's mind was set on heaven. To him, this was much more than a proper doctrine of heaven, but it ran through his veins to give oxygen to his body and soul. It comes alive in his familiar passage to the Philippians in Chapter 3: "Not that I have already attained, or am already perfected; but I press on, that I may lay hold of that for which Christ Jesus has also laid hold of me. Brethren, I do not count myself to have apprehended; but one thing *I do*, forgetting those things which are behind and reaching forward to those things which are ahead, I press toward the goal for the prize of the upward call of God in Christ Jesus" (verses 12-14).

We can only surmise what Paul's life would have been without his revelation of heaven. Although I have heard a few testimonies similar to Paul's, most of us have not experienced a visitation to heaven. This is where our faith must reach out with certainty and take hold of this wonderful, eternal future we have. Paul tells the Corinthians that the Holy Spirit is our guarantee, or down payment on this marvelous future. (See 2 Corinthians 5:1-8). For most of us, we need to exercise ourselves in training our minds heavenward. In order to imitate Paul, this is an indispensable opportunity to rise above the issues of life.

I want to share a final word about faith. Life and ministry have taught me that personal faith is a precious thing. It is a valuable gift from God, and is not to be taken for granted. It must be protected, cared for and fed. Do not take your faith for granted. The enemy would love to attack it.

Be careful of what you say and do. Be careful of how you speak about God and about your circumstances. Feed your faith with the Word of God. Do not allow the enemy to plant seeds of doubt and unbelief; take those thoughts captive. Faith is like a garden — it must be watered and fed with good fertilizer, pruned, and protected from every predator. A garden will yield abundant fruit when in the hands of a loving and knowledgeable gardener. Cultivate your garden of faith carefully.

A Right Relationship To Trials

The third component of endurance is being rightly related to trials. The importance of this matter cannot be overstated. God can use the trials of life for great good; Satan can use them for terrible destruction. The choice is up to us.

I know far too many Christians who have allowed contrary circumstances and the trials of life to batter their faith and erode their walk with God. Some have completely fallen away from following Jesus.

Paul, our powerful model as a church planter, is also the premier example in Scripture of a man who was *rightly related to trials*. Right relationship with trials is an interesting and important matter. It is particularly relevant to discipleship. Jesus told us to go into the entire world and make disciples. Many churches endeavor to have discipleship programs with the purpose of growing mature believers into fully formed disciples of Christ.

A study of Scripture will reveal that there are four powerful elements that, when properly woven together, will produce a disciple. A disciple is formed, not from taking a discipleship class, but by participating actively in these four ingredients in the course of life. It is a magic recipe yielding the mature disciple.

- Trials
- The Word of God
- The Spirit of God
- Faith

When the trials of life are faithfully combined with the Word (living and active), administered by the Spirit, and mixed with your faith, you grow into a strong, mature disciple of Christ. This is God's program for making disciples.

Let's look at two passages of Scripture that shine a light on this subject.

My brethren, count it all joy when you fall into various trials, knowing that the testing of your faith produces patience [endurance]. But let patience [endurance] have its perfect work, that you may be perfect [mature] and complete, lacking nothing (Js. 1:2-4).

Therefore, having been justified by faith, we have peace with God through our Lord Jesus Christ, through whom also we have access by faith into this grace in which we stand, and rejoice in hope of the glory of God. And not only *that*, but we also glory in tribulations, knowing that tribulation produces perseverance; and perseverance, character; and character, hope. Now hope does not disappoint, because the love of God has been poured out in our hearts by the Holy Spirit who was given to us (Rom. 5:1-5).

Notice in James 1:2 it says "count it all joy." It does not say to *enjoy* the trials! *Count* is a mathematical term, so it means that you know the formula, so to speak. You know that $a + b = c$, or in context, you know that trials + faith = endurance, and endurance + time = a mature, complete Christian who lacks nothing. Neither James nor Paul is saying we should enjoy a trial or tribulation; only that we should remain under them, not run away, stay on our post, and know what they will produce in our lives. We are able to glory in them because we know God is involved and we are in a process he is overseeing, for our ultimate good.

Thankfully, the New Testament documents Paul's life in significant detail. We see the trials he went through and the final result they produced in his life. Time and time again Paul rejoices in the midst of his trials and writes to his churches about them. Paul was who he was because of the trials he went through. We see him singing behind bars and writing some of his most powerful and hopeful letters from prison.

For the church planter, the church leader, and every other believer, trials are an essential component to your character, your faith, and ultimately to your ministry. You do not grow strong in faith in a classroom. I would assert that you cannot become a person of great faith without great trials. You do not obtain great character by birth, nor by attending bible college or seminary. Faith, character, and maturity are grown and strengthened in the school of trials.

When the trials of life and ministry come your way, if you stay in the Word of God, enjoy the fellowship of the Holy Spirit, and believe that God is actively working in your life in the midst of everything, you will grow strong in faith and become a great man or woman of God. Endurance will become an essential asset in your life and you will finish your race with joy. It is a bit like the illustration — a brown cow eats green grass and produces white milk — I don't understand how it works, but it does.

Trials are part of God's preparing you for your ministry. When I graduated from bible college I remember thinking that because I had obeyed God and finished my schooling I was now ready to pastor God's sheep. I was in for a huge surprise! God knew differently. I was shocked to find that I had to make a major detour, in fact two detours. I have since learned that, with God, the shortest distance between two points is *not* a straight line! He had things I needed to learn and experience in those detours that could be learned no other way. Trials, delays, pressures, and disappointments — all planned by God for my good and his glory. But I did not give up during these detours because I was certain of my calling.

Do not be surprised if your life will be characterized by detours that become major trials.

My experience was a mirror image of God's plan to train and equip the children of Israel after they passed through the Red Sea and embarked on their journey to the Promised Land. Notice what Moses tells us in Exodus 13:17-18:

> Then it came to pass, when Pharaoh had let the people go, that God did not lead them by way of the land of the Philistines, although that was near; for God said, "Lest perhaps the people change their minds when they see war, and return to Egypt." So God led the people around by way of the wilderness of the Red Sea. And the children of Israel went up in orderly ranks out of the land of Egypt.

God intentionally did not lead the nation of Israel directly to the land of Canaan via the most direct route. He knew they needed to learn important lessons before they encountered the giants in the land. The time in the desert exposed their weaknesses and sins, as trials do for each of us — unbelief, fear, murmuring, self-pity, insecurity, pride, and self-dependence to name just a few. God is still doing this today and you and I are not exempt from a time in the desert. It is one of the ways of God with his children.

My wife and I have cherished for many years what David says in Psalm 103:7, "He made known His ways to Moses, His acts to the children of Israel." We have prayed and asked the Lord to show us his ways, not just his acts. This can be a dangerous prayer! One of the principle ways of God (valuable knowledge especially for church planters to know as you start out) is that he may close doors you thought would open, leading you on a circuitous route. There may be tests and challenges in the detour that are necessary for you to fulfill your destiny. Do not murmur as the Israelites did, but rejoice and respond in faith.

God can use trials to bring us to the end of ourselves. This is one of his ways. It may seem painful at the time, but there is a goal: "I have been crucified with Christ; it is no longer I who live, but Christ lives in me; and the *life* which I now live in the flesh I live by faith in the Son of God, who loved me and gave Himself for me" (Gal. 2:20). The power and anointing we see operating in Paul's life and ministry is not because of the strength of Paul himself, but the power of the resurrected Christ working through a completely yielded vessel. If you are going through painful circumstances now, seemingly abandoned in the desert, maybe God is using them to bring you to the end of yourself, able to say, *not I but Christ.*

This now leads us logically to a very important matter. If we are to be rightly related to trials we must understand this. The Israelites were blind as to what God was doing when he did not take them directly to the Land of Promise. *God had an agenda they were unaware of.* He knew things they did not know. He could see what was in their heart and they were not prepared to fight and win the battles that awaited them in Canaan. His promise to the Jews that they would return to Canaan from Egypt was certain. (Gen. 15:12-16). Verse 16 tells us something very important: "But in the fourth generation they [the Israelites, Abraham's seed] shall return here [Canaan], for the iniquity of the Amorites is not yet complete." God was allowing the Israelites remain in slavery in Egypt until the sins of the Amorites were full.

This has significant implications for every Christian. It is natural to assume we know what God is doing in our lives and ministries. Often these expectations are based on what we want to happen, not necessarily what is on God's mind at that particular time. You might think God is doing "x" in this season of your life, but what if he is doing "y"? If your expectations are based on God doing "x" and he doesn't, you may become confused and discouraged. Maybe you are going through a crisis right now. What is God doing? Are you sure? Maybe he is doing something in your character. Maybe he is building your faith. Maybe he is delaying in order for other matters to happen that you are unaware of. Maybe your vision is too small and he is preparing you for greater matters. Maybe he is redirecting you.

In Isaiah 55:8-9, God says, "For My thoughts are not your thoughts, nor are your ways My ways. For as the heavens are higher than the earth, so are My ways higher than your ways, and My thoughts than your thoughts." We see this principle working in the life of Hannah in 1 Samuel 1-2. Hannah was suffering inconsolably because she could not bear a child. Why? What was wrong with her? Where was God? Chapter 1 verse 6 tells us God closed her womb. God wanted a Samuel. Israel needed a Samuel. Through this intense trial of suffering Hannah willingly surrendered her baby boy to the Lord. God was doing something of which Hannah and her husband were unaware.

We see this principle operating in Paul's life. He was in prison suffering unjustly. Why? What did he do wrong? Where was God? God used Paul's imprisonment for great good: for the furtherance of the gospel; for much prayer for his churches; as a place to write his prison epistles.

God is still the same. He may be doing things in your life and ministry you do not yet fully understand. Your sufferings and trials may be part of a greater plan than you can currently see. You have a choice. Choose to trust him and finish your race with joy even if you do not fully understand what is going on. Look beyond circumstances and believe God. Let's explore this more fully.

A Choice

Trials present to every Christian a choice of how to respond. The first is to intentionally react according to the Word of God, believing and trusting the process detailed in James 1:2-4 and Romans 5:1-5. This takes faith that God is working in the situation for good. This is the spiritual response. When you can rejoice in a trial, you are responding in faith. God has called you to be a spiritual person, living and responding according to the ways and principles of the Kingdom.

Look closely at James 1:4 again. "But let patience [endurance] have its perfect work, that you may be perfect [mature] and complete, lacking nothing." Notice that James says we are to *let* patience have its perfect work. This is where you get to decide how to react to adversities. If you respond in faith you will enable (allow) the trial to have its way in you — becoming perfect, complete, lacking nothing. Biblically speaking this can be summarized in one word — LOVE. I can assure you, if you respond properly, the sufferings and trials will tenderize your heart and make you a man or woman of love. If you let them, trials destroy pride and self-confidence and produce a sweet smelling aroma in your character. Some of the sweetest, loving people I have known are those who have suffered the most. The choice is yours – will trials produce a sweetness or a bitterness?

The second option is to respond in a natural or carnal way. Depending on the type of trial, there are many possible responses, including, but not limited to, fear, doubt, anger, hurt, resentment, bitterness, unbelief, unforgiveness, self-pity, and condemnation. These responses are easy to understand in the natural but are contrary to God's Word and will sow seeds of destruction in your life and ministry. These responses provide access to the devil to work in your life and destroy what God wants to build.

The central matter is your heart. Proverbs 4:23 says, "Keep your heart with all diligence, for out of it spring the issues of life." The New Living Translation puts it this way: "Above all else, guard your heart, for everything you do flows from it."

This Scripture holds a key, at least in part, as to why so many Christian lives deteriorate, why church planters fail, and church leaders quit. Hearts can become scarred by trials — cold, resentful, and bitter. It is very important to guard your heart and watch over it carefully, for everything you do flows from it. Your ministry will largely be dependent upon how you respond to trials.

This choice you will have to make over and over in your life and ministry. Again, we see a parallel with the children of Israel during the ministry of Moses. At the close of Deuteronomy, Moses is warning Israel to follow God. He tells them of the blessings if they do and the curses if they do not. Then comes this powerful statement in Deuteronomy 30:19, "I call heaven and earth as witnesses today against you, that I have set before you life and death, blessing and cursing; therefore *choose life*, that both you and your descendants may live." Choose life. This remains a crucial decision for you today in your ministry. Choose to respond to trials in accordance with Kingdom principles, not worldly values. Choose life.

Let's take this one step further for church planters and leaders. We learn something important from Paul's life and the times in which he lived. Paul had a spiritual understanding of the trials he experienced. He was not surprised at what happened to him. He was not caught off guard.

Most of Paul's trials came at the hands of the Jewish religious leaders and zealots. The primary issue of Paul's day was the relationship of the New Covenant to Jews and Gentiles. Paul understood this clearly and was not taken by surprise. The Lord taught him deep truths about the one new man, Jew and Gentile, one in Christ.

Paul developed this teaching for his readers, especially in Romans and Ephesians. Because he understood what was going on, he was not surprised when the majority of Jews rejected the gospel. It was all part of God's plan to take the gospel to the Gentiles (Rom. 11:25-29). False teachers going into his churches teaching legalism did not surprise him. He was not surprised when he was thrown in prison. Paul was not inclined towards self-pity and quitting when circumstances were bearing down on him because he had an understanding of the big picture and how his life and ministry clashed with the culture of his day.

This is concept can be helpful to us today. When we have an awareness of the most prevalent trials of our age, we are able to respond to them positively. When we don't understand the big picture they often defeat us. So, what are the more common trials experienced by church leaders today? The list is long, but would certainly include these: stress due to time pressure and expectations, financial pressures, opposition to your leadership, disunity, feelings of betrayal as people move from church to church, worldliness, relativism, narcissism, and many more. Do not be surprised by these things. It is part of the ministry. Rejoice and allow them to work in you endurance, enabling you to finish your race with joy. Do not co-labor with the devil to allow discouragement to defeat you.

Endeavor to be rightly related to trials, responding in faith. Don't keep asking, "Why is this happening to me?" Refrain from murmuring. Allow them to mature you, growing in your "Paul-likeness." Do not let them make you bitter or fill you with resentment. This may become the greatest decision you will ever make. Imitate Paul.

I often tell believers it is not so much how you start your Christian walk but how you finish. It is not so much how your walk with God is now, but how you end your race. Endurance is like the rebar that is put into a concrete structure giving it strength and support that will last many years, withstanding all the forces and stresses placed on it.

I want to make an important distinction here between trials and tragedies. In what I discussed above I am not speaking of personal, heart breaking tragedies, such as sudden or premature death of loved ones, tragic accidents, diseases, etc. Additionally there are natural disasters on a global scale resulting in massive casualties. Growing numbers of believers are being martyred for their faith, many of which are broadcast before our eyes. These are not the trials Paul and James are speaking about when they say, "count it all joy when you fall into various trials."

Tragedies are trials, but all trials are not tragedies.

For victims of tragedies, we weep with those who weep. Unfortunately, in a fallen world, bad things happen to good people. They just do. The devil will use tragedies to try to destroy your faith. But, God is still God. He is good and he has a plan for your life. He may not answer the whys of the situation, but he will comfort, restore, and build you up again. The calling on your life is still the same — to finish your race with joy and the ministry you have been given. Do not give up. Never never never give up. God will give you the grace needed to carry on.

I find one Scripture particularly helpful in these matters. When John the Baptist was in prison (soon to be beheaded by Herod), he sent two of his disciples to Jesus asking, "Are You the Coming One, or do we look for another? 'Jesus answered and said to them, 'Go and tell John the things which you hear and see: The blind see and the lame walk; the lepers are cleansed and the deaf hear; the dead are raised up and the poor have the gospel preached to them. *And blessed is he who is not offended because of Me'"* (Matt. 11:3-6, emphasis mine).

Here is what was going on. John was Jesus' cousin. He baptized him. He saw the Holy Spirit descend on Jesus. Surely he knew Jesus was the Messiah, the "Coming One." John's dilemma was this: Jesus was performing miracles everywhere, and he knew John was in prison. Why would Jesus not do something to get him out and save his life? *Surely he would,* John must have been thinking. Jesus' answer was less than John would have wanted, but is very instructive for all of us 2000 years later. Jesus was saying, "Blessed is he who is not caused to stumble ("turn away," NLT) because of me." In other words, blessed is he who does not stumble or turn away *when I do not do what he thinks I should do.*

Life may have brought times when you thought God would do something and he didn't. You may be hurt, disappointed, and angry with God. That's OK, but take Jesus' words to heart. You will be blessed if you do not fall away because of it. The message of this chapter and this book, all from Paul's life, does not change — do not quit, finish your race with joy.

Now, back to trials, not tragedies. I want to share one final word about trials that has helped me immensely. It is a natural response to trials to ask, *Why? What have I done wrong? Why is this happening? Where is God in all this? What can I change to get out of this?* It is natural, and not necessarily wrong, to ask questions. (Keep in mind though, that Paul and James exhort us to rejoice in trials, knowing their purpose and process.) Yes, perhaps there are things that need to be changed and repented of. And yes, perhaps there are matters that need to be made right. Without going too deep into the source and theology of trials and suffering though, let me highlight one aspect of this from Paul's life, from 2 Corinthians chapter 11.

In this chapter Paul was defending his true apostleship against false apostles. One would think Paul would list his accomplishments in defending himself, but no, he boasts of his sufferings! His sufferings and trials are in fact his *credentials* as an apostle. Let me say that again. Paul lists his sufferings as *credentials* in his ministry. You can read his list of trials in verses 22-33. Paul did nothing wrong and did not bring the sufferings on himself. They validated his true ministry and his righteous living before the churches.

Paul goes even further in Colossians 1:24, where he says, "I am glad when I suffer for you in my body, for I am participating in the sufferings of Christ that continue for his body, the church" (NLT). As a follower of Jesus, our sufferings become a mark of authenticity in our lives. Suffering is part of leading a church, and is part of being a believer in the midst of a fallen and God-hating world. Rejoice! You are the real deal.

Questions to consider:

1. Spiritually speaking, do you consider yourself better at sprinting or long distance running? Do you quit easily when things get hard? Why?
2. Think about how important endurance is in your Christian life. What alterations in your thinking are necessary?

3. Evaluate your ministry and marriage with respect to love versus duty. Are there things you can do to re-fire your passions?

4. As an exercise to build your faith, read through Hebrews 11 every day this week. Think of the times when you have exercised your faith. Can you see yourself included in the list of Hebrews 11?

5. How do you currently view trials? Do you feel you are rightly or wrongly related to them?

6. Have you ever experienced a time when you thought God was doing "x" when he was doing "y"? Perhaps that could help explain your current circumstances.

7. Are you co-laboring with the devil or with God in your response to trials? Why don't you consider rejoicing and praising God in the midst of your current tribulations? Can you see any way God can use them for your good?

8. Do a bible study on 1 Peter 1:3-9. How real is your hope in heaven? (See also Rom. 8:23-25, 15:13; Heb. 6:18-19). How can this idea change your life?

9. How has this chapter encouraged you to develop endurance? Do you see things in your life, historically and currently, with a new perspective?

10. Looking back on your life, can you see God at work in your trials, building your faith and developing endurance?

11. Read these verses over carefully and let them give you the courage to continue on no matter what your current situation is: Hebrews 2:1, 6:11-12, 10:36-39; 1 Corinthians 9:24-27.

CHAPTER 7

A Secret Place

We move now to the fifth key in Paul's life that was critical to his success as he defined it — to finish his race with joy and the ministry he had been given by Jesus. Paul gives us only one verse on this key, but it is an insightful and exciting window into his private life with God. Even though it is only one verse, we need to give special attention to it, especially because of the context in which this verse appears.

> Therefore we do not lose heart. Even though our outward man is perishing, *yet the inward man is being renewed day by day.* For our light affliction, which is but for a moment, is working for us a far more exceeding and eternal weight of glory, while we do not look at the things which are seen, but at the things which are not seen. For the things which are seen are temporary, but the things which are not seen are eternal (2 Cor. 4:16-18, emphasis mine).

Paul is putting the afflictions he has suffered into an eternal perspective. His afflictions affected his outward man but his inward man was being renewed day by day. Daily

Paul's soul was being refreshed and renewed. He was drawing not from this world's resources, but from heaven's.

This matter we have before us is something most Christians have been taught from the beginning of their Christian lives. We call it by many terms – devotions and quiet time, to name just two. Even mentioning this subject brings feelings of guilt and condemnation to countless believers, including church leaders. We know we should spend time alone with God. It is, of course, important and the right thing to do, but in the demands of life and ministry, it too often falls down our list of priorities.

So, I launch out in this final key to Paul's success knowing many of my readers will have preconceived ideas and lifelong experiences of failure. You may even be tempted to skim over this chapter thinking you have heard it all before. Please don't. This may be the most important of Paul's five keys. "So why," you may ask, "did you leave this as the final chapter?" Often we remember most what we read last.

The ONE Thing

My experience has not been different from what I just described. Things, however, are changing in my own life. I recently read a non-Christian book that dramatically affected my understanding of Paul's secret place with the Lord. I was browsing books in the airport as I was waiting for my flight to depart. Suddenly one book caught my attention. You know what it's like when something seemingly "jumps into your hands!" Sensing this was an important book for me to read, I immediately downloaded it onto my Kindle from the airport's wifi network and began to read on the flight home. I was not disappointed. Although it is not a Christian book, I became excited as I saw its application to my own life and the teaching of Scripture. God was using this book to open my eyes to previously unseen things.

The book is "The ONE Thing" with the subtitle, "The Surprisingly Simple Truth Behind Extraordinary Results" by Gary Keller, with Jay Papasan.[1] Although he never mentions Jesus, Keller lays bare a simple truth that Jesus taught when he told Mary and Martha in Luke 10:41-42, "... Martha, Martha, you are worried and troubled about many things. But *one thing* is needed, and Mary has chosen that good part, which will not be taken away from her" (emphasis added).

So, what is the concept behind this book, "The ONE Thing?" It is simply this. "When you want the absolute best chance to succeed at anything you want, your approach should always be the same. Go small. 'Going small' is ignoring all the things you could do and doing what you should do. It's recognizing that not all things matter equally. It's realizing that extraordinary results are directly determined by how narrow you can make your focus. Unaware that big success comes when we do a few things well, they get lost trying to do too much and in the end accomplish too little."[2]

The smaller the focus, the greater the possibilities. Becoming accomplished at multi-tasking is usually applauded and sought after. Keller, however, argues that this is the exact wrong approach. He suggests one should become focused on the ONE thing that is the most important and spend an inordinate amount of time and energy on that activity. "Selected effort creates almost all of the rewards. The majority of what you want will come from the minority of what you do. Extraordinary results are disproportionately created by fewer actions than most realize."[3]

Keller has developed a focus question that he suggests should be asked for all situations. "What's the ONE Thing I can do such that by doing it everything else will be easier or unnecessary?"[4] I have come to see that this is exactly what can happen when Christians make their secret place with God their ONE Thing. This is the only thing that will make everything else easier or unnecessary. This is what Jesus meant when he taught about the vine and the branches in John 15. "Abide in Me, and I in you. As the branch cannot bear fruit of itself, unless it abides in the vine, neither can you, unless you abide in Me. I am the vine, you are the branches. He who abides in Me, and I in him, bears much fruit; *for without Me you can do nothing*" (emphasis mine).

This is the point of Jesus discussion with Mary and Martha. Martha was distracted with many things; very good things – personally serving Jesus and his disciples. The life of a Christian (especially leaders) is characterized by an exhaustive list of good and seemingly necessary activities. There are never ending demands on our time. Never enough time to do everything or please everyone. Keller quotes an old Russian proverb to help drive home his point. "If you chase two rabbits you will catch neither." By the nature of the job, Christian leaders are chasing many rabbits; juggling priorities, solving problems, counseling, guiding and leading ministries, preparing sermons, developing leaders, etc.

For many Christians our daily time set aside to seek the Lord has become one more task squeezed into an already crowded schedule; something to be ticked off our to-do list before we scamper off into a fast-paced world trying to be productive. A quick internet search will reveal a plethora of apps and tools to more efficiently manage our list of duties and activities. Effective time management is a huge topic. The world is trying to manage greater and greater demands with increasing pressure to perform.

Keller's book has caused me to think deeper about this subject. We know of course, in general terms, that living according to the ways the Kingdom of God is different from living according to the ways of the world. What if this also applies to time management? What if God has set up a plan and a way of living that provides a different approach to leading a church or ministry, planting a church, or simply living the Christian life? What if Paul truly found the secret? What if a time set aside to sit at Jesus' feet (like Mary) is the ONE thing that could be done that would make everything else easier or not necessary at all? This is an exciting possibility. This becomes a paradigm shift in the way we think of our time with the Lord in the secret place.

Keller uses a powerful illustration of dominos to illustrate his thesis.[5] We all know what is meant by a *domino effect*. As children we would set up a long line of dominos, standing on end, and watch with amazement as we carefully knocked down the first domino and observed as all the others rapidly fall. This simple children's pastime has become a worldwide phenomenon. Contests and challenges have arisen all over the world using millions of dominos creating spectacular displays of creativity.

Keller's point is this. "When one thing, the right thing, is set in motion, it can topple many things."[6] He goes on to describe how there is a geometric progression, that as the falling dominos gain momentum they are able to topple larger and heavier dominos. The application of this concept to Jesus' teaching and Kingdom living opens up new possibilities in the way we spend our time and in the way we look at productivity.

Consider what might change in life's issues and challenges if we made the decision that our first domino was our *secret place* with God, enjoying the love of the Father, the grace of Jesus, and the fellowship of the Holy Spirit. If we centered our lives around focusing on this one priority, this one domino, perhaps we would find other dominos falling and gaining momentum — the Lord providing answers and solutions to problems, peace and joy replacing stress and worry, burdens lifted, mountains moved, resources provided, relational issues resolved, anointed sermons coming more easily, etc.

Kingdom Living

For most Christians this will take a paradigm shift; a shift from this set aside time being something we try to wedge into our schedule, to the ONE thing that empowers and enables everything else in life and ministry to be effective. Most believers understand that the ways of Kingdom living are juxtaposed against the ways of the world. These lifestyles of the Kingdom are explained by Jesus in Matthew chapters 5-7. To mention just a few: we live a life of forgiveness, refraining from judging, giving generously, being merciful, turning the other cheek, fasting and praying, doing to others as we would have them do to us, and so forth. We are called to this lifestyle as Christians. Kingdom living brings blessing, fruitfulness, joy and peace (along with persecution). The nine fruits of the Holy Spirit flow from a life lived in a Kingdom way.

I am suggesting there is also a Kingdom principle operating in the way we spend time, order our day, and accomplish great things for God; a Kingdom approach to time management that is different from the world's ways. When a divine connection is cultivated every day heaven's resources begin to flow into your life. Dominos begin to fall. Other tasks become easier or unnecessary. As Christians, let us bring our priorities and time management under the same umbrella of Kingdom principles as the other areas of a Godly lifestyle. Paul evidently practiced this and it became a foundation in his life of victory.

As we have seen, Paul's soul was renewed daily. Let's go a little deeper — renewed from what ... to what? What needed renewing and what was it renewed to? The context seems to make this clear. Paul's many afflictions (see 2 Corinthians 11:23-33 for a summary) and the heavy burdens of ministry undoubtedly had an effect on him as a man. He must have dealt with things such as weariness, worry, stress, anxiety, disappointment, discouragement, unforgiveness, fear, rejection and self-pity – all encouraging him to lose heart. The issues of life take their toll.

What would his soul be renewed to? Jesus begins to open this up to us in his wonderful promise in Matthew 11:28-30: "Come to Me, all *you* who labor and are heavy laden, and I will give you rest. Take My yoke upon you and learn from Me, for I am gentle and lowly in heart, and you will find rest for your souls. For My yoke *is* easy and My burden is light." This is a special promise of rest for those who are weary from much work and exhausted from carrying heavy loads on their back. The word rest could also be translated refresh or revitalize. It is apparent that Paul developed a daily practice of going to Jesus, unloading his burdens, and having his soul refreshed and revitalized. He began every day at rest.

Additionally, Paul would take time to reset his thinking, from temporal matters to heavenly promises. Paul writes in 2 Corinthians 4:18 "... while we do not look at the things which are seen, but at the things which are not seen. For the things which are seen are temporary, but the things which are not seen are eternal." Daily circumstances, problems, and issues can easily dominate our thoughts, devour our time, and crush our spirit. They weigh us down and wear us out. They eat away at our joy, at our peace, and test our faith. To combat this, Paul daily reset his vision from earthly to heavenly. He knew that he was only passing through this life on earth to his final destination. He set his heart not so much on the journey and its challenges, but the destination. To imitate Paul, we too need to daily recalibrate our faith and thinking to focus on our heavenly destination.

Based on Paul's other writings, I believe we are safe in saying he was renewed in the fruit of the Holy Spirit. Paul lists nine fruits of the Spirit in Galatians 5:22-23: "But the fruit of the Spirit is love, joy, peace, longsuffering, kindness, goodness, faithfulness, gentleness, self-control." Try to imagine what it would be like to begin every day afresh and anew with these nine fruits. We would become joyful overcomers. We would be victorious in the midst of the trials of life. Paul must have developed his secret time with the Lord going through a process of appropriating his words in 2 Corinthians 5:17, "...old things have passed away; behold, all things have become new."

This daily transformation was an irreplaceable component in Paul's life. Is it any wonder that a key strategy of the devil is to keep us busy, distract us, and wear us out so that we try to live life and serve God on empty? Most, if not all of us, have fallen victim to this, victim to the tyranny of work and busyness. Many of us have become slaves to a work ethic that devours our time and energy. God speaks to the quiet heart; to the son our daughter who sets aside quality time to be with him in a time of fellowship and intimacy. Is this not a key explanation of the difference between the lofty promises of Scripture and the spiritually sub-par lives we see around us?

A.W. Tozer catches the heart of what I believe Paul found as a secret of his life and ministry. "The world is perishing for a lack of knowledge of God and the Church is famishing for want of His presence."[7] Once again, Tozer has captured the essence of Paul's secret in few words.

The secret place is a place of the presence of God. "Repent, therefore and be converted, that your sins may be blotted out, so that times of refreshing may come from the presence of the Lord" (Acts 3:19). Your soul will become refreshed when you spend time in his presence – refreshed with joy and peace. David tells us in Psalm 16:11: "You will show me the path of life; in your presence is fullness of joy; at Your right hand are pleasures forevermore." As you will remember, Paul's vision was to finish his race with joy. In light of the tribulations of life and ministry, there is only one source of lasting joy – spending time daily in God's presence, receiving directly from the Word and the Spirit.

Peace is a gift of God also. He is the God of peace. Paul says in Colossians 3:15 "And let the peace of God rule in your heart ..." My friend, what is ruling your heart today? It is God's desire that every son and daughter live in a state of peace, yet this seems to be the first thing to go in the day-to-day ministry of church planters and leaders. Peace has been God's desire for his children from the beginning. This is at the heart of the prayer he gave to Aaron and his sons to bless the children of Israel: "The Lord bless you and keep you; The Lord make His face shine upon you, and be gracious to you; The Lord lift up His countenance upon you, and give you peace" (Num. 6:24-27). It is the Father's heart to bless you with his peace. This is available to you every day.

The *secret place* is also where the Lord will give you the knowledge and wisdom needed to carry out your life and ministry. Set aside the time and quiet your soul. Unload your burdens and seek his wisdom and direction. Jesus did what he saw the Father doing (Jn. 5:19-20). Your quiet time is a place to seek him for wisdom, direction, and priorities; to see, as Jesus did, what the Father is doing in your life and ministry.

Notice that Paul does not tell us his "strategy." We do not know the formula for his inward man to be renewed day by day. Undoubtedly Paul's time included praise, prayer, confession, declaration and reading the Scriptures. However, for our purposes here, discovering his method is not the relevant matter. It is not the method that is important, but the relationship he developed and the daily renewing he received. It is all too easy to fall into the trap of the Galatians,

beginning in the Spirit, but trying to be made perfect by the flesh.
A formula would soon lead to obeying a set of rules and
standards to please God (See Galatians 3). Perhaps best of all,
we should set aside time to be in his presence with no agenda
other than communion with God, cultivating our relationship
with him. No prayer requests, no complaints, not trying to be
productive – just fellowship time with our Father, our Savior,
and the Holy Spirit.

Paul, living in the first century, had one significant
advantage over us living in the twenty first century — the
simplicity of life. Even in my lifetime I can look back and see
how much simpler life was growing up in the 1950's and
1960's. Today life is busy, complicated, and full of distrac-
tions. It is difficult to live life without emails and the internet,
without fixing broken cars and rusted bicycles, without bal-
ancing bank accounts and paying bills. Our children need to
be taken to soccer practice and dancing lessons. The list is
endless. Yet, Paul's secret remains unchanged. We must set
priorities and make first things first. This is Kingdom time
management and Kingdom priorities. When we push hard on
this first domino, others will fall.

We see Jesus regularly getting away for times of fellowship with his father and fresh fillings of the Holy Spirit.
"So He Himself often withdrew into the wilderness and
prayed" (Lu. 5:16). Jesus offers this to us as well. He taught in
John 15 that he is the vine and we are the branches; that we
are to abide, or rest in him. When we do, the life-giving sap
will flow into the branches. This is the only way we can continue to have the life of Christ alive in us, and the only way
we can continue to be filled with the fullness of God (Eph.
3:19). Without this daily infusion of life-giving sap we will

become dry and brittle. This is something we can all attest to, I'm sure.

I have always admired the writings of Andrew Murray. They have encouraged and challenged me many times. Perhaps one of the keys to his life and writings can be captured by the first part of his "Daily Fellowship with God."[8]

> The first and chief need of our Christian life is, *Fellowship with God*. The Divine life within us comes from God, and is entirely dependent upon Him. As I need every moment afresh the air to breathe, as the sun every moment afresh sends down its light, so it is only in direct living communication with God that my soul can be strong.
>
> The manna of one day was corrupt when the next day came. I must every day have fresh grace from heaven, and I obtain it only in direct waiting upon God Himself. Begin each day by tarrying before God, and letting Him touch you. Take time to meet God. To this end, let your first act in your devotion be a setting yourself still before God.

Murray talks about having a "living communication with God." Communication. Most of the readers of this book have grown up with the idea and practice that communication happens through email, Facebook, texting, Snapchat, and Twitter! Social media has altered what it means to have fellowship and communicate. Just observe two people having a meal together – usually fiddling with their phones instead of engaging face to face. Let's be careful that we don't bring over these social media habits and expect to have the blessings of God found only as we abide in his presence.

Set aside a block of time. Block out everything else so this time with Jesus will be the ONE thing, the domino that will begin a chain reaction. It seems to me that God's love language is quality time!⁹

Hezekiah's Tunnel

I want to give you a wonderful picture of this from an archeological discovery in Jerusalem in combination with Psalm 46. My wife and I have been to Israel many times. On one of those trips we included a tour through Hezekiah's tunnel. This was a fascinating walk back in history 2700 years.

First, let's review some background to understand the historical context. You can read about the construction of this tunnel in 2 Kings 20:20 and 2 Chronicles 32:30. In preparing Jerusalem for an enemy invasion in about 700 B.C., King Hezekiah redirected the water supply of the city. Jerusalem's main water source was from a natural spring called Gihon Spring, which was situated outside the city walls. Because of its location it was vulnerable to capture. It would have been easy for an enemy to cut off the city's water supply, thereby leading to their rapid defeat. Without water Jerusalem could not hold out for long.

Hezekiah had his men dig a tunnel through bedrock 1,750 feet long well below the earth's surface in order to divert the water. This was a significant engineering and construction feat for those times. The tunnel was discovered in 1838 and was cleared of all debris in 1910. It has now been made available to tourists who can walk through parts of it, often wading in knee-deep water.

Warfare in those times involved long sieges against walled cities, cutting off food and water supplies. We see instances of this throughout Scripture. (You can read the fascinating story of King Hezekiah's preparations for the enemy siege in Isaiah 36-37.) Ancient survival strategies included the protection of the water supply and long-term storage of food. King Hezekiah was therefore arranging provision of a life-giving supply of water to the inhabitants of Jerusalem when the enemies of Israel would lay siege to the city. *The enemy could lay siege to the city but had no access to the source of life. They could bang on the walls, but could not cut off the water.*

Now let's turn to Psalm 46:1-7, and we will see a powerful truth that points forward to John 7:37-39 when Jesus stood at the pool of Siloam (where the water from Hezekiah's tunnel emptied) on the last day of Tabernacles.

God is our refuge and strength,
A very present help in trouble.
Therefore we will not fear,
Even though the earth be removed,
And though the mountains be carried into the midst of the sea;
Though its waters roar and be troubled,
Though the mountains shake with its swelling.   Selah

There is a river whose streams shall make glad the city of God,
The holy place of the tabernacle of the Most High.
God is in the midst of her, she shall not be moved;
God shall help her, just at the break of dawn.
The nations raged, the kingdoms were moved;
He uttered His voice, the earth melted.

The Lord of hosts is with us;
The God of Jacob is our refuge.   Selah

We see in verse 1 the psalmist is addressing a pressing time of trouble. Verses 2 and 3 describe the trouble in earthshaking, mountain-moving terms, yet the psalmist says "Therefore we will not fear" because God is with us. How is he with us? This is spelled out in verse 4 — "There is a river whose streams shall make glad the city of God, the holy place of the tabernacle of the Most High."

This is alluding to Hezekiah's tunnel bringing a supply of fresh water into the city of God (Jerusalem), where the tabernacle of the Most High resides. The result – making the city glad. The water of life was flowing even though the Assyrian army was laying siege to the city walls.

Now let us turn to the fulfillment of this Old Testament typology. As a follower of Jesus you are now the temple of God, the tabernacle of the Most High. Even if earthshaking, mountain-moving troubles assault you, there is a source of life available to you, springing up on the inside, that the enemy has no access to!

No matter what trial or tribulation you are going through, or will ever experience, there is a free flowing source of life, strength, power, grace, and wisdom that cannot be stopped. The enemy may shake you up and bang on the walls of your life, but he cannot cut off your supply of the water of life. This source of water *never* runs dry. Psalm 65:9 tells us, "The river of God is full of water."

Let's turn to the New Testament. In John 7:37-39, Jesus stood up on the last day of the feast of Tabernacles, at the very place where Hezekiah's tunnel emptied into the pool of Siloam, and cried out these powerful words:

> On the last day, that great day of the feast, Jesus stood and cried out, saying, "If anyone thirsts, let him come to Me and drink. He who believes in Me, as the Scripture has said, out of his heart will flow rivers of living water." But this He spoke concerning the Spirit, whom those believing in Him would receive; for the Holy Spirit was not yet given, because Jesus was not yet glorified.

Spiritually speaking, the Apostle Paul drank at this pool daily. He was refreshed and empowered by the Spirit that raised Jesus from the dead. Let's look again at Paul's prayer in Ephesians 3:14-21 with this idea in mind:

> For this reason I bow my knees to the Father of our Lord Jesus Christ, from whom the whole family in heaven and earth is named, that He would grant you, according to the riches of His glory, to be strengthened with might *through His Spirit in the inner man*, that Christ may dwell in your hearts through faith; that you, being rooted and grounded in love, may be able to comprehend with all the saints what is the width and length and depth and height—to know the love of Christ which passes knowledge; *that you may be filled with all the fullness of God*. Now to Him who is able to do exceedingly abundantly above all that we ask or think, *according to the power that works in us*, to Him be glory in the church by Christ Jesus to all generations, forever and ever. Amen (emphasis mine).

This is Paul's prayer for us. Paul experienced this daily and wants you to be filled as well — filled and strengthened with might (Gr. *dunamis*) in our inner man, filled and overflowing with his presence, his love, and the fullness of God. As a result we are able to do more than we could ever imagine because of the power that works in and through us. My friend, this is a keystone for victorious Christian living. This was an irreplaceable aspect of Paul's life. Let us imitate Paul.

This is more than merely having our daily devotions, at least in the way I think of that term. I suspect this phrase, daily devotions, has become a *cliché*. (def. "... a phrase, usually expressing a popular or common thought or idea, that has lost originality, ingenuity, and impact by long overuse..."[10] It is more than reading our bible daily. It is more than squeezing in a short time of prayer before the day gets going. Yes, it may include all of these of course, but Jesus and Paul used terminology that suggests a refreshing drink of water for a thirsty soul and a fresh filling with power to live our lives and fulfill our ministries. Surely it suggests an intimate daily time with our Father, abiding in Jesus, sitting at his feet, and the fellowship and fresh filling with the Holy Spirit. Surely it includes repenting of our sins and laying at the feet of Jesus all of our worries and concerns and allowing him to carry them.

This idea of intimacy is confirmed with Jesus' words in Matthew 6:6. "But you, when you pray, go into your room, and when you have shut your door, pray to your Father who is in the secret place; and your Father who sees in secret will reward you openly." The word *room* here in the NKJV is taken from the Greek word *tameion,* which is translated as *closet* in the King James Version.

This Greek word has an interesting historical progression. At first, it was used to depict a secret place where one would hide his or her most valuable possessions. It then came to describe a secure place where a person could put money or treasure, and by New Testament times it came to describe a bedroom. This is because a bedroom is a secret place where husband and wife share their most intimate relationship. So Jesus is saying that we are to go into our most secret place to share our deepest matters with our Father. This is a protected place where our inner man is renewed, filled, and replenished daily.[11]

Biblical Meditation

There is another topic that may prove helpful in developing your own secret place and refreshing time with God. This has proven to be invaluable to me over the years. In the late 80's, my wife gave me a birthday present — a weekend resident course on *biblical meditation*. A well-known Christian ministry in Britain was hosting this course. Little did I know at the time that this experience would set me on a life changing-adventure.

To continue our theme of water, let's look briefly at Psalm 1:1-3:

Blessed is the man
Who walks not in the counsel of the ungodly,
Nor stands in the path of sinners,
Nor sits in the seat of the scornful;

But his delight is in the law of the Lord,
And *in His law he meditates day and night.*

He shall be like a tree
Planted by the rivers of water,
That brings forth its fruit in its season,
Whose leaf also shall not wither;
And whatever he does shall prosper (emphasis mine).

Every believer should be excited to be compared to a tree that is planted beside a river — always green, fruitful, and prospering in all he does. What a promise. There are two conditions given in this passage: first, not to walk in the ways of the ungodly, and second, to delight in and *meditate* on the Word of God.

In the weekend course I was taught about biblical meditation — what it is, how to do it, and how it changes our lives. I will only give the briefest outline here. You can pursue this further on your own.

First, in case this is a new subject to you, it is important to say that this has nothing whatsoever to do with any type of Eastern religion or New Age meditation you might have heard about. As I understand it, that type of meditation involves emptying your mind. This can be dangerous and ought never to be done. On the other hand, biblical meditation involves filling your mind with the Word of God.

Meditating on Scripture has blessed me immensely and changed my life. Very simply, I pick a verse or a passage of Scripture that is important to me or seems to be prompted by the Lord. I write it on a card and memorize it. Once I memorize it I begin to chew on it. By this, I mean that I go over it in my mind and heart, thinking about each word or phrase, picturing what it means and how it applies to my life. As I am memorizing it, I try to bring it into my mind throughout the day. After it is fully embedded in my mind, I use this as a launching point for praise and prayer.

If part of your life or character is weak and needs strengthening, choose Scripture that is the antidote. For instance, if you are fearful, find Scripture that is relevant, such as 2 Timothy 1:7. If you want more love in your life, then pick Scripture about love, like 1 Corinthians 13:4-8. If you are weak in faith, pick key verses from Hebrews 11 or Romans 4, for example. If you are struggling with a sin, Romans 6 is a powerful place to start. Memorize these passages and begin to meditate on them, rolling them over in your mind and heart, praying them and proclaiming them.

Don't forget, the Word of God is living and active. As you *feed* on the Word, you will receive life and nourishment. God will use it to transform you, renew your mind, and change your heart. Proverbs 4:23 tells us, "Keep your heart with all diligence, for out of it spring the issues of life." The heart is the source which "...determines the course of your life" (NLT). Paul picks up on this theme in Romans 12:2 where he tells us not to be conformed to this world "...but be transformed by the renewing of your mind..."

Much of what I am sharing in this book has come from memorizing and meditating on Paul's prayers in Ephesians 1 and 3. They have been an unspeakable blessing to me. Years ago I wrote Ephesians 3:14-21 on cards and memorized them while on a two week family vacation. I took those cards everywhere with me. It was quite a challenge but the rewards were rich. I received more refreshment from that exercise than I did from two weeks on a beach holiday!

I have done this for so long now that I automatically meditate on some of my favorite Scriptures as I go to bed at night and when I first awake in the morning. It brings joy and peace to my heart and refreshes my soul. This is a wonderful alternative to what many people do at night — worry.

I find it interesting to speculate on Paul's life in light of this idea. As a Pharisee of Pharisees and a scholar, he was brought up in Tarsus at the feet of Gamaliel, the famous Jewish Rabbi. We know almost certainly that Paul had much, if not all, of the Old Testament memorized. I wonder, did Jesus, through the Spirit, open the eyes of his understanding as he pondered, chewed, and meditated on many of the Scriptures he had learned? Was his inner man renewed daily as he did this? Perhaps.

The Apostle Paul, thankfully, included 2 Corinthians 4:16 in his writings to us. It gives a glimpse into his life with God — Father, Son, and Holy Spirit. "Therefore we do not lose heart. Even though our outward man is perishing, yet the inward man is being renewed day by day."

Like so many Christians, I have not done as well as I had wanted in imitating Paul. I do fine for a while, but then seem to drop back. Perhaps part of the reason is that I do not realize how much God desires to spend time with me. "We love him because he first loved us" (1 Jn. 4:19).

James seems to be saying this in chapter 4 verse 5: "Or do you think that the Scripture says in vain, 'The Spirit who dwells in us yearns jealously?'" In context James is saying that when we switch our allegiance to the world, the Spirit yearns jealously. When the Greek word for *yearns* is understood in more depth, this verse is stunning.

The Greek word *epipotheo* is translated as *yearns* in the NKJV. This word portrays an intense desire, a craving, a hunger, an ache, a longing or pining for something — an intense, abnormal, excessive yearning. This is like a drug addict who is craving a drug fix, saying "I *must* have it. Give me what I need, now."[12] But here in James 4 it is describing the Holy Spirit as craving each of us. He does not want to share us with the world. He craves to have fellowship with us. He needs a fix!

This reminds me of an amazing testimony I first heard many years ago from my good friend Dr. Don Crum. Don was on a ministry trip leading an important series of meetings in the northwestern part of the US. He arrived at his hotel on a Friday afternoon. As the first meeting was not until Sunday morning, Don requested to be left alone until then. He felt an unction to spend this time privately with the Lord. He spent Friday night, Saturday, and Sunday morning in his hotel praying, fasting, and worshipping. He never left his room. As Don relayed the story to me, it was a special time, sensing and feeling a strong presence of God with him.

Saturday night at 11:00 p.m. he went to bed expecting to get a good night's rest before beginning the meetings Sunday morning. However, God had different plans. At exactly 12:00 midnight he was awakened and heard the Holy Spirit say to his heart, "Can we have just a few more minutes together?" Very surprised and in awe, he got up and spent a few minutes in worship and prayer, until about 12:30 p.m. when he went back to bed and fell asleep.

At exactly 1:00 a.m., he was again awakened as the Spirit whispered into his heart the same thing, "Can we have a few more minutes together?" Again he got out of bed and spent time worshipping and praying, falling back in bed at 1:30 a.m.

Then came 2:00 a.m., — you guessed it. He was awakened exactly on the hour with the same request, "Can we have just a few more minutes together?" Every hour on the hour until 5:00 a.m. this happened. There was a digital clock on the nightstand, and each time it was exactly on the hour, :00.

Needless to say, this was a life altering experience for my friend. He had never experienced such a divine presence, like a heavy cloud, resting upon him and filling his hotel room. The love he felt was tangible. Although this only happened on this one occasion, it is a window into the heart of God for each of us.

Surely God is the Divine Lover. The fruit of the Holy Spirit is love. Jesus is the lover of our soul. If we could only get a revelation of how great his love is toward us — not only in a historical event (the cross), but in daily living. The Holy Spirit yearns, even craves for your heart and your time. He cannot get enough of you! Imagine that.

I am confident that Paul developed a lifestyle of spending time in the *secret place* with the Lord. Out of this place of intimacy came everything we observe in his life — his love for God and for his churches, his joy in and through all circumstances, his knowing that Christ was dwelling in his heart, his inner man filled with might through the Spirit, yes, even filled with the fullness of God. Paul's life was fueled and oiled by the presence and power of God. We see this in his writings and in his prayers for you and me, especially in Ephesians 3:14-21.

Paul's Prayer

I want to encourage you to try meditating on each phrase in Ephesians 3:14-21. I am convinced that Paul is praying for us exactly what he experienced in his own secret place with Jesus. He is praying for you personally. This is not just for apostles or prophets, but also for you and me. Begin to take this prayer personally, praying and receiving all it has for you. Let this be the center of your secret place with the Lord. Memorize each phrase and go over it in your mind and heart. Picture what it is saying to you personally. Apply it to your life. Use it as a launching point for prayer and proclamation.

- "I bow my knees to the Father..."
- "That he would grant you..."
- "According to the riches of His glory..."
- "To be strengthened with might through His Spirit in the inner man..."
- "That Christ would dwell in your hearts by faith..."
- "That you, being rooted and grounded in love ..."
- "May be able to comprehend ..."
- "What is the width and length and depth and height..."
- "To know the love of Christ which passes knowledge..."
- "That you may be filled with all the fullness of God."
- "Now to Him who is able to do exceeding abundantly above all that we ask or think..."
- "According to the power that works in us..."
- "To Him be glory in the church by Christ Jesus..."
- "Throughout all ages, world without end, Amen."

My prayer is that you will launch out into the deep of a more intimate relationship with the Father, the Son, and the Holy Spirit. May your secret place become a daily time of refreshing and empowering. May the Lord *grant you*, according to the riches of his glory, all the spiritual riches freely given to you as his son or daughter.

Word and Spirit

As I said earlier in this chapter, I won't try to suggest a formula because Paul does not offer one. It is not about formulas, it is about relationship. If we make it into a formula it becomes a duty. We want it to be the result of a relationship born out of love.

However, there is a principle that needs to be highlighted. Whatever Paul did in conducting his private relationship with God it would have included both the Word of God and the Holy Spirit. *Word and Spirit.* My observation over the years is that many believers and churches alike tend to major on one, not both. There seem to be churches that focus heavily on the Word at the expense of the Spirit and others that emphasize the Holy Spirit at the expense of the Word.

Paul's writings are a wonderful balance of both the Word and the Spirit. He never seems to emphasize one to the exclusion of the other. Right after Paul writes, "let the peace of God rule in your hearts" in Colossians 3:15 (which is a fruit of the Holy Spirit), he writes in verse 16, "Let the word of Christ dwell in you richly..." To be a victorious, overcoming Christian like Paul it is imperative that we have a healthy balance of both the Word and the Spirit. We must be strong, knowledgeable, and grounded in the Scriptures and at the same time filled with the Holy Spirit, daily cultivating an intimate fellowship with him, and drinking from the river of God.

Questions to consider:

1. What does it mean to you personally, to have your inward man renewed day by day? Have you experienced this? Assess you own daily devotional time in light of this chapter.

2. Considering this idea of focusing on the ONE thing, how would you evaluate your personal time management? Can you see how the domino effect might have a positive impact on your effectiveness? (See also Ps. 27:4-5).

3. Do you identify more with Martha or Mary? What are the consequences?

4. Why is peace such a valuable asset to the believer? Look at these verses (Is. 26:3, Jn. 14:27, 16:33, 2 Cor. 13:11, Phil. 4:4-9, 2 Thess. 3:16) and Paul's use of it in the armor of God in Ephesians 6:15. How does peace give the spiritual soldier solid footing?

5. If you agree with the philosophy of the ONE thing, why not experiment with it for 30 days? Block out generous time and focus on the primary domino.

6. Do the problems of your life capture more of your attention than the promises of heaven awaiting you? Why not begin to change your focus?

7. Do you believe God would say to you, "Can we have just a few more minutes together?" Are you con-

vinced he loves you this much? (See also Song of Solomon 5:2-6.)

8. Challenge yourself to this experiment. Write Ephesians 3:14-21 on cards or a piece of paper. Go over it until you are very familiar with it, even committing it to memory. Then take each phrase, one at a time, and begin to meditate on it. Talk to God about each phrase and how it applies to your life. Try doing this as you fall asleep at night and awake in the morning.

9. Take time to honestly evaluate this idea of Word and Spirit in your life. If you are a church leader, how would you assess your church? Write down two changes to make that would re-balance your life and ministry.

10. Set aside time this week to read through Scripture slowly in a meditative way. Here are places you might consider: Isaiah 55; Song of Solomon 2; Psalm 1, 23, 27, 42, 63.

CHAPTER 8

An Eternal
Imperative

We have examined five keys to the Apostle Paul's life that are often overlooked and undervalued. Whether taken individually or collectively, they contribute to a Christian life worthy of the Lord. They contribute to a life such as Paul displayed before us — a life of faithfulness, fruitfulness, and victory all the way to the end.

Life can be fraught with trials and tribulations, as was Paul's. As we get deeper into the last days and closer to the coming of Christ, I believe we will see an increasing amount of shaking in the earth. In Matthew 24 Jesus answers the disciples' questions, "And what will be the sign of Your coming, and the end of the age?" (Matt. 24:3b). After revealing some signs he says in verse 8 "All these are the beginning of sorrows." The NIV translates sorrows as birth pangs. As the

161

birth of the baby nears the birth pangs get stronger and closer together.

In Hebrews 12:26-29, the writer emphasizes this theme of shaking:

> ... whose voice then shook the earth; but now He has promised, saying, "Yet once more I shake not only the earth, but also heaven." Now this, "Yet once more," indicates the removal of those things that are being shaken, as of things that are made, that the things which cannot be shaken may remain. Therefore, since we are receiving a kingdom which cannot be shaken, let us have grace, by which we may serve God acceptably with reverence and godly fear. For our God is a consuming fire.

Everything will be shaken, that can be shaken. There will be an obvious distinction between those things that cannot be shaken and those that can. Our Christian lives must be built on solid ground, or on a rock, as Jesus said. As we look at the condition of the body of Christ in this hour, we must be concerned. Are we made of the same material as our Christian ancestors like Paul? Do we have the same faith, grit and determination? Are we ready for Christ's coming?

Jesus was not hesitant to talk about the critical importance of watching and being ready and awake for his return.

> "But take heed to yourselves, lest your hearts be weighed down with carousing, drunkenness, and cares of this life, and that Day come on you unexpectedly. For it will come as a snare on all those who dwell on the face of the whole earth. *Watch therefore,* and pray always that you may be counted worthy to escape all these things that will come to

pass, and to stand before the Son of Man" (Lu. 21:34-36, emphasis mine).

In his discourse in Matthew 25, Jesus goes into much more depth as to what he expects in the days just prior to his second coming. He gives illustrations of the days of Noah in verses 36-44, and of two servants in verses 45-51. This is followed by the parables of the Ten Virgins and the Talents. The theme is consistent — be awake, ready, and on the front foot in the things of God. Jesus' words are important and urgent. We need to take his warnings seriously.

Jesus' exhortations and warnings to the seven churches in Revelation 2-3 are often overlooked as well. To each of the seven churches he exhorts them to *overcome*:

To the church of Ephesus: "To him who *overcomes* I will give to eat from the tree of life, which is in the midst of the Paradise of God" (Rev. 2:7, emphasis mine).

To the church of Smyrna: "He who has an ear, let him hear what the Spirit says to the churches. He who *overcomes* shall not be hurt by the second death" (Rev. 2:11, emphasis mine).

To the church of Pergamos: "He who has an ear, let him hear what the Spirit says to the churches. To him who *overcomes* I will give some of the hidden manna to eat. And I will give him a white stone, and on the stone a new name written which no one knows except him who receives it" (Rev. 2:17, emphasis mine).

To the church of Thyatira: "And he who *overcomes*, and keeps My works until the end, to him I will give power over the nations" (Rev. 2:26, emphasis mine).

To the church of Sardis: "He who *overcomes* shall be clothed in white garments, and I will not blot out his name from the Book of Life; but I will confess his name before My Father and before His angels" (Rev. 3:5, emphasis mine).

To the church of Philadelphia: "He who *overcomes*, I will make him a pillar in the temple of My God, and he shall go out no more. And I will write on him the name of My God and the name of the city of My God, the New Jerusalem, which comes down out of heaven from My God. And I will write on him My new name" (Rev. 3:12, emphasis mine).

To the church of Laodicea: "To him who *overcomes* I will grant to sit with Me on My throne, as I also overcame and sat down with My Father on His throne" (Rev. 3:21, emphasis mine).

Without exception Jesus says the church must *overcome*. Seven times! You can be certain that Jesus, after repeating the same phrase seven times, is serious. This is an important and urgent matter for every believer to embrace. Church leaders must prepare their people to be overcomers.

Yes, these five keys I have highlighted from Paul's life are important for the church planter and church leader, enabling them to have every possibility of success in their ministry, and in fulfilling their destiny. They are important for every Christian, as well, to live their lives and fulfill their callings. Each one of you has a calling, a purpose, and a destiny.

God has a plan for your life. "For we are His workmanship, created in Christ Jesus for good works, which God prepared beforehand that we should walk in them" (Eph. 2:10). Many things must be overcome to fulfill your destiny and calling — trials, disappointments, opposition, and most of all, yourself. You contain within yourself much that must be overcome — your weaknesses, sins, bondages, etc. You need everything Paul had in order to be an overcomer; to finish your race with joy and the ministry you have been given.

I want to end this book with a compelling message. These five keys are *not* simply nice add-ons to your Christian life and ministry. In light of Jesus' warnings, they take on an added urgency, even an eternal perspective. They are essential ingredients to every believer's life to finish the race with joy; to be ready and awake for the return of Christ. Without these I am fearful for the bride of Christ that she will be shaken beyond recognition in the last days. Paul was the preeminent overcomer and we are able to glean from his life and writings those attributes that enabled him to be so successful.

A Final Review

Here is one last review of the five keys to Paul's victorious life that we observe from his life and writings.

A Certain Calling: Paul never doubted his calling. He was sure and certain. When life and ministry take twists and turns you must be certain of God's call on your life. You must know your purpose. When the devil whispers into your ears, *Hath God said?* you are able to shout back, *God hath said!* You can then turn your back on him and his lies, and get on with it. *Imitate Paul.*

A Lasting Vision: Paul set his eyes on the finish line and his vision is a must for all followers of Jesus: "But none of these things move me; nor do I count my life dear to myself, so that I may finish my race with joy, and the ministry which I received from the Lord Jesus, to testify to the gospel of the grace of God" (Acts 20:24). Paul was not so much interested in short-term results, as they can lead to pride and self-exaltation if things go well, or to discouragement and defeat if they do not. If too much hope is placed in them, you are set up as a prime target for the devil. *Imitate Paul.*

A Personal Revelation of the Glorious Gospel: The grace and power that comes from the gospel is released as it becomes personal revelation. The power to live the Christian life in all its biblical strength and power, overcoming everything, being joyful and fruitful, comes from the power of God himself living in and through you — "filled with the fullness of God" (Father, Son, and Holy Spirit).

A useful metaphor for the gospel is like a multi-faceted diamond – one diamond but many facets, each one reflecting the beauty and glory of the stone itself. This beautiful gospel provides the answer, encouragement, strength, strategy, and grace for every circumstance of life and ministry. One of the most powerful and least practiced aspect is the three-step progression Paul develops in the book of Ephesians – sit, walk, and stand. First we must sit, receiving all our spiritual blessings we have been given by grace. Secondly, our Christian walk is the outworking of our spiritual riches in Christ (who we have become in Christ), and finally we are equipped to stand against the enemy and his strategies. There is the Kingdom way of living which is contrary to the world's way of living. Choose the Kingdom order, receiving by grace everything you have been given. Personal revelation is the key to closing the gap between the lofty promises of Scripture and the experience of many. *Imitate Paul.*

A Strong Finish: Endurance is not merely an apostolic gift given to Jesus' disciples in biblical times, but is an essential ingredient for all believers. It develops in all our lives as we learn three important lessons of life in the Kingdom of God. First, our motive must be love, not duty. Lovers work harder and do not burn out. The second and third elements of endurance go together to create character and maturity — a biblical response to trials and strong faith. When trials are responded to properly, Scripture says that you will become mature, complete, lacking nothing (Js. 1:2-4). *Imitate Paul.*

A Secret Place: Even though we have become the temple of the Holy Spirit, we are still made of flesh and blood. We need to be filled daily as we set aside a secret time and place with God (Father, Son, and Holy Spirit). Paul's inner man was renewed daily. This activity needs to become the ONE thing that has priority over all others. Without this daily refreshing and empowering of the Word and the Spirit, we will dry up and wear out. *Imitate Paul.*

Conclusion of the Matter

We began this book with Paul's vision – to overcome every trial, every obstacle, and finish his race with joy and the ministry he had been given. How did he do? Did he accomplish his vision?

Paul ran his race all the way to the end, motivated to receive his crown — an imperishable crown of righteousness. Paul was anticipating Jesus' words, "Well done, good and faithful servant; you were faithful over a few things, I will make you ruler over many things. Enter into the joy of your lord" (Matt. 25:21).

Here, in his final letter to his faithful son in the ministry, are these words to Timothy:

> The time of my departure is at hand. I have fought the good fight, I have finished the race, I have kept the faith. Finally, there is laid up for me the crown of righteousness, which the Lord, the righteous Judge, will give to me on that Day, and not to me only but also to all who have loved His appearing (2 Tim. 4:6-8).

May you too be able to imitate Paul in his closing words — his graduation speech before he was promoted to heaven.

Notes

Introduction

1. Taken from pastoralcareinc.com,
    http://www.pastoralcareinc.com/statistics/, statistics
    provided from The Fuller Institute, George Barna, and
    Pastoral Care Inc. **NOTE:** These statistics and others like
    them can be found easily on the internet. Most of these
    statistics are dated, many being 10-20 years old. Some
    statistics are gathered at large gatherings and may not be
    statistically significant. This book is not trying to use
    them in a definitive way, but simply as a way of demon-
    strating what is generally accepted — the challenges, tri-
    als, and casualty rates among church leaders is
    significant. A real problem exists.

Chapter 1: A Significant Problem

1. pastoralcareinc.com; statistics provided from The Fuller
    Institute, George Barna, and Pastoral Care Inc. See **NOTE**
    above under Introduction.

Chapter 2: A Certain Calling

1. Darrin Patrick, *Church Planter, The Man, The Message,
    The Mission,* (Wheaton, Ill.: Crossway, 2010), 29-40.
    Used by permission of Crossway, a publishing ministry
    of Good News Publishers, Wheaton, IL
    60187, www.crossway.org. This is an excellent book that

develops more thoroughly the ideas and concepts behind the church planter himself. I recommend this book
for further study.

2. Dr. Miles Munroe, *In Pursuit Of Purpose, The Key To Per-
    sonal Fulfillment,* (Shippensburg, PA: Destiny Image Pub-
    lishers, Inc., 2015), 156. Reprinted with permission.

3. Rick Renner, *Sparkling Gems from the Greek. Vol. I,*
    (Teach All Nations, 2003), 77, February 8 reading. Re-
    printed with permission.

Chapter 3: A Lasting Vision

1. A.W. Tozer, *God's Pursuit of Man,* (Camp Hill, PA: Wing
    Spread Publishers). Used with permission, fair use.

2. Renner, *Sparkling Gems I*, 146, March 10 reading.

3. John Beeden blog, *It Was Never Going To Be Easy,*
    www.solopacificrow.com; September 28 entry,
    http://solopacificrow.com/2015/09/29/it-was-never-
    going-to-be-easy/.

Chapter 4: A Personal Revelation

1. "Revelation,"EastonBibleDictionary.com,
    http://eastonsbibledictionary.org/3119- Revelation.php.

2. Renner, *Sparkling Gems I*, 39, January 21 reading.

3. Spirit Life Bible, Copyright© 2002 by Thomas Nelson,
    Inc.

4. Derek Prince, *Extravagant Love*, Kindle Book, in his
    teaching on Romans 8:15-17.

5. L.B. Cowman, *Steams In The Desert*; Devotional reading
    for Feb. 29. Used with permission.

6. Mary Stewart Relfe, Ph.D. *"Cure Of All Ills"* (Montgomery, AL: League of Prayer, 1988).

Chapter 5: A Glorious Gospel

1. Renner, *Sparkling Gems I*, p. 130, March 3 reading.
2. Watchman Nee, *Sit, Walk, Stand*, ©1977. Used by permission of Tyndale House Publishers, Inc. All rights reserved.
3. A.W. Tozer, *The Knowledge of the Holy*, (New York: Harper Collins, 1961), *1, 2*.
4. This verse, 2 Corinthians 5:21 is a powerful truth for the deity of Christ. This verse alone should give every Jehovah's Witness great pause for thought. It alone tears the heart out of a false doctrine of Christ. Let's carefully look at the pronouns in this verse. "For He [God] made Him [Christ] who knew no sin to be sin for us, that we might become the righteousness of God in Him [Christ]." This is often called the "exchange at the cross." Jesus took upon himself our sins and in turn gave to us his righteousness. This verse tells us Christ's righteousness is in fact the righteousness of God (Theos). If Christ were anything less than fully God he could not have given us the righteousness of God himself.
5. Cowman, *Streams*, September 27 reading.
6. A.W. Tozer, *God's Pursuit of Man* (Camp Hill, PA: Wing Spread Publishers), Ch. 5. Fair use permission granted by Moody Publishers.
7. Renner, *Sparkling Gems I*, 111, February 23 reading.
8. Renner, *Sparkling Gems I*, 139, March 7 reading.
9. Jonathan Cahn, *The Book of Mysteries* (600 Rinehart Road, Lake Mary FL. 32746, FrontLine, Charisma Media/Charisma House Book Group;

www.charismahouse.com) Day 48 reading. Reprinted with permission.

Chapter 6: A Strong Finish

1. "Freeny Takes It All," *IPC Swimming*, https://www.paralympic.org/feature/freney-takes-it-all (30 April 2016).
2. Renner, *Sparkling Gems I*, 146, March 10 reading.
3. The reason our financial pressures were such a test of faith was that my visa (Minister of the Gospel) prohibited any work outside the church. Many church planters will have part-time or full-time jobs when the church is in its early stages.

Chapter 7: A Secret Place

1. Gary Keller and Jay Papasan *The ONE Thing: The Surprisingly Simple Truth Behind Extraordinary Results*, (Austin, TX: Bard Press, 2013; www.the1thing.com). Reprinted by permission. Although not written from a Christian perspective, the concepts presented are powerful in their scriptural application.
2. Keller, *The ONE Thing*, p. 10.
3. Keller, *The ONE Thing*, p. 37-38.
4. Keller, *The ONE Thing*, Ch. 10.
5. Keller, *The ONE Thing*, Ch. 2.
6. Keller, *The ONE Thing*, p. 13.
7. A.W. Tozer, *The Pursuit of God: The Human Thirst For The Divine*, (Start Publishing, eBook edition, October 2012), p. 36.

8. *Andrew Murray Collection; The Deeper Christian Life,* p. 1; Copyright © 2014 Cary M. White.

9. "Quality time" is one of the five love languages that Gary Chapman discusses in his book, *The 5 Love Languages: The Secret to Love that Lasts*; Northfield Publishing.

10. Cliché. (n.d.). Dictionary.com. *Dictionary.com Unabridged*. Random House, Inc. http://www.dictionary.com/browse/cliche (accessed: January 12, 2017).

11. Renner, *Sparkling Gems I*, p. 571; August 7 reading.

12. Renner, *Sparkling Gems I*, p. 91-92; February 14 reading.